1

A BATTLE THAT EVEN KINGS LOST
WINNING YOUR OWN BATTLE
FOR SEXUAL PURITY

Dr. Raul F. Moreno, D. Min.

A Battle That Even Kings Lost:
Winning Your Own Battle For Sexual Purity

Cover design by José Otero

ISBN-13: 978-1723023743 (createSpace-Assigned)
ISBN-10: 1723023744

FORWARD

One of the greatest blessings of the kingdom is my friendship with Raul Moreno. It began in earnest in January 2005, when Lynda and Raul were in Santiago, Chile and they visited Elena and me in Portland, Oregon. It was at that tumultuous time in our fellowship of churches that they humbly asked for us to disciple them, yet we are the ones that 13 years later have learned so much more from them.

Raul reminds me of the Apostle Nathanael – *"in whom there is nothing false."* Raul is the Sir Galahad of the World Sector Leaders Roundtable – whose gallantry, purity and love for Campus Ministry is an upward call to all. From my favorite movie, *Gladiator*, Raul is Maximus – the Roman General whose integrity was severely tested by ungodly persecution and who said, "What we do in life echos in eternity."

Raul's first of prayerfully many books, *A Battle That Even Kings Lost – Winning Your Own Battle For Sexual Purity* is not merely the newest classic from SoldOut Press International, but it's message "will echo in eternity." In this book, Raul addresses many controversial issues that face disciples every day, while candidly describing his battles – lost and won – against Satan in Raul's quest for sexual purity. He draws out the Scriptures to not only give us hope that we too can be decisively victorious in the arena of sexual purity, but

Raul gives several radical practicals that have worked for him to remain pure both before and after marriage in the kingdom.

In closing, *A Battle That Even Kings Lost* strengthened my walk even at 64 years old. My prayer is for our gracious Father to use this precious book so that so many more may enter heaven dressed in our *"white robes"* of purity. And to God be all the glory!

Kip McKean
August 2, 2018

CONTENTS

PART FOUR   **SPECIFIC BATTLES**

Introduction
Even Kings Lose Battles

What do King David, King Solomon and the Judge of Israel, Samson, have in common? All three of them damaged their lives and the lives of those they led because they minimized, and thus ignored, their lusts and sexual sin.

David sinned by lusting after Bathsheba. (2 Samuel 11:2-4) That lust led to adultery, deceit, drunkenness and ultimately murder. It had a profound effect on his kingship, his family, his mighty men and all of God's people.

Solomon's all-consuming lust led him to a destructive sexual desire that not even 700 wives and 300 concubines could quench. (1 Kings 11:3) As an old man, one of the consequences of this sin was that he worshipped other gods: Ashtoreth, the goddess of the Sidonians; Chemosh, the detestable god of the Moabites; and Molech of the Ammonites, the god worshipped through baby human sacrifices. It also led God to split the kingdom after his death, never to be rejoined. (1Kings 11:9-13)

Samson's lust led him into the sin of marrying a non-Israelite woman (Judges 14:1-3), sex with a prostitute (Judges 16:1), and an immoral relationship with the Philistine Delilah. This ended with his demise. The loss of his hair, which represented his covenant with God, led to the loss of his supernatural strength, which led to the loss of his eyes, his vision, which led to the loss of his freedom and honor as he became a slave to the Philistines all of which emboldened the enemies of Israel to mock God. Ultimately, Samson's lust and sexual sin cost him his very life.

The man after God's own heart, the wisest man in the world and the strongest man in the world were taken out by lust and sexual sin. Here is a sobering lesson for all of us. Lust and sexual sin are "every man's battle," and the same can be said for most women. As disciples of Jesus, we are in the world but not of the world John 17:16. Jesus said, *"Blessed are the pure in heart for [only] they will see God."* Matthew 5:8. If this pervasive temptation of lust and sexual sin is not challenged from the pulpit, disciples of Jesus will not make it to heaven, and the wrath of God will come upon them here and beyond. (Ecclesiastes 5:3-7)

A great question to ask is: Why is there so much sexual sin in the world?

Here is a Scripture to consider:

> *The wrath of God is being revealed from heaven against all the godlessness and wickedness of people, who suppress the truth by their wickedness, since what may be known about God is plain to them, because God has made it plain to them. For since the creation of the world, God's invisible qualities – His eternal power and divine nature – have been clearly*

seen, being understood from what has been made, so that people are without excuse. (Romans 1:18-20)

According to this Scripture, there is no excuse for not following God. There is enough evidence in nature for everyone to seek God. Therefore, atheists and agnostics have no real argument before God about not following him. When we persist in not following God, he sends his wrath. His wrath is his punishment and discipline towards those who do insist on disobeying him. However, all punishment and discipline from God have one purpose: To bring us back to him. (Psalm 119:71, Romans 2:4) Unfortunately, when people suffer, most choose to flee from God even more. (Revelation 16:9)

Humans were made to worship! When we do not worship God, we begin to "worship" other things. This is what we call idolatry, and it is the natural progression of sin as we see in the following passage:

For although they knew God, they neither glorified him as God nor gave thanks to him, but their thinking became futile and their foolish hearts were darkened. Although they claimed to be wise, they became fools and exchanged the glory of the immortal God for images made to look like a mortal human being and birds and animals and reptiles. (Romans 1:21-23)

11

Since we are made to worship, we will worship idols when we are not worshipping God. In the context of the first-century church, they worshipped other false gods. In the 21st century, in the Western Hemisphere, our idols can be somewhat different but equally damaging. They can be such things as sex, money, success, sports, entertainment, material possessions, relationships, power and the like. This is what happens to man when man decides not to follow God:

> *Therefore, God gave them over in the sinful desires of their hearts to sexual impurity for the degrading of their bodies with one another. They exchanged the truth about God for a lie, and worshipped and served created things rather than the Creator – who is forever praised. Amen*
>
> *Because of this, God gave them over to shameful lusts. Even their women exchanged natural sexual relations for unnatural ones. In the same way, the men also abandoned natural relations with women and were inflamed with lust for one another. Men committed shameful acts with other men, and received in themselves the due penalty for their error. (Romans 1:24-27)*

This is an amazing passage that clarifies an incredible principle for us: **"God gives us over."** Over to what? What does this phrase mean? It means this: If we insist on sinning sexually, there is going to come a point where it becomes an idol in our lives. Why? Because we love it more than God. After a certain point of persisting in this sin, God gives us over to it even more. God gives us over to the point where we now are addicted and most likely, will have a struggle with this sin for the rest of our lives. This happens with sexual sin. Most of us have been given over by God to this sin because we decided to indulge in it consistently as non-Christians. In actual fact, this passage also says that sexual impurity is something God deliberately gave people over to, implying that when we lose sight of God in the first place, one of the most common things we will turn to is sexual sin.

If we persist in lusting, watching pornography and masturbation, God will give us over to this sin. That is why so many people have a deep problem with these sins. The same thing applies to sexual immorality and homosexuality. According to this Scripture, God gives us over to homosexuality when we persist in it. No one is born homosexual according to the Bible. It is not an issue of genetics. It is an issue of obedience (more on this subject in a later chapter).

So how is "God's wrath" displayed, as it is stated in Romans 1? God's wrath is shown in the fact that he gives us over to sin when we decide to persist in it. God gets tired of us sinning, and he punishes us and disciplines us by giving us over. This is why there is so much sexual sin in the world. Sexual sin is, perhaps, the most common sin that most men and many women decide to give themselves to the most.

Of course, this principle applies to all sin and not just

sexual sin. For example, if we persist in alcohol and drugs, there will come a point when God will give us over and we will become an addict and have a lifelong battle with this.

The same thing goes for other sins like pride, anger, bitterness, hate, lying, greed, insecurity, etc.

So what happens after God gives us over to a sin? Is there any hope? Are we doomed after this? Can we change? The answer is a resounding yes! We can change. With God, we can change anything! But in order to do that, we must first understand a spiritual principle:

> *Therefore, in order to keep me from being conceited, I was given a thorn in my flesh, a messenger of Satan, to torment me. Three times I pleaded with the Lord to take it away from me. But he said to me, "My grace is sufficient for you, for my power is made perfect in weakness." Therefore, I will boast all the more gladly about my weaknesses, so that Christ's power may rest on me. That is why, for Christ's sake, I delight in weaknesses, in insults, in hardships, in persecutions, in difficulties. For when I am weak, then I am strong. (2 Corinthians 12:7-10)*

God knew that the Apostle Paul struggled with pride. Because of that, God gave him a "thorn in the flesh" that made him weak. The Bible does not say what this "thorn" was, and this is good because we can all relate to Paul in this sense. It could have been a disease or eye problems or a character weakness or maybe something else. God kept Paul's pride under control by giving him a weakness. This weakness made Paul needy! In his weakness, he relied on God and not on himself! Thus, through this thorn, Paul remained God's instrument and did not give himself to his pride! So therefore, his life-long struggle with pride actually drew him nearer and nearer to the cross, as he allowed God to strengthen him through this weakness. So instead of a life-sentence of condemnation, through grace, we have a life-long promise of victory.

Likewise, when God gives us over to sin, like sexual sin, it is a tremendous weakness in our lives. Like Paul's thorn, it was meant to be like that. Why? So that we would rely on God and not on ourselves. If we have been given over to sexual sin, it is probably something we battle on a daily basis. Since we are or have been a slave to this sin, the only hope we have of overcoming is God.

To rely on God, we first have to understand God's goodness. This is the spiritual principle that we must learn and persist in understanding in all facets of our lives! We have to understand that God is good! (Psalm 106:1) That means that even his discipline is good for us, as Hebrews 12:5-7 says:

> *And have you completely forgotten this word of encouragement that addresses you as a father addresses*

his son? It says,
"My son, do not make light of the Lord's
discipline, And do not lose heart when
he rebukes you, because the Lord
disciplines the one he loves, And he
chastens everyone he accepts as his
son."
Endure hardship as discipline; God is
treating you as his children. For what
children are not disciplined by their
father?

When God disciplines us and we suffer, it is because he loves us. When God gives us over to sexual sin, it happens because he loves us. It is not pleasant or fun. But if we train in righteousness, we will be able to overcome this sin. This is what this book is all about.

A Battle That Even Kings Lost – Winning You Own Battle For Sexual Purity is the title of this book, but also God's warning for our lives. We must not ignore this battle, but rather fight with all our might. There are no character weaknesses or sins that we cannot overcome with God. Prayerfully, the Scriptures outlined in this book will persuade you that this life-changing perspective is God's all throughout the Scriptures!

This book will explore how to overcome the battle of sexual sin in our lives. Part One of the book is entitled, *The Losing Battle*, in which we will see what happens when sexual sin has defeated us and its dire consequences. Part Two is entitled, *The Battle Of The Heart.* In this section, we will study biblical principles of how to overcome, at a heart level, as well as practical advice to engage our hearts in the battle every day. Part Three is entitled, *The Battle Of The Mind.* We will look at how we can train our minds through the Scriptures. Practicals will also be given in this section. Finally, part Four is entitled, *Specific Battles.* Here, we will look at several difficult battle grounds for sexual purity and how to gain the victory through spiritual training and godly wisdom.

My prayer is that in the ensuing pages, God can better equip you not only to fight this battle but be victorious, as we gloriously await Jesus's coming! Until then, let us *"shine like stars"* and give Jesus glory! (Philippians 2:15) I hope you enjoy the journey as much as I have!

Part One
The Losing Battle

Chapter 1
Occupation By The Enemy

It is God's will that you should be sanctified: that you should avoid sexual immorality, that each of you should learn to control your own body in a way that is holy and honorable, not in passionate lust like the pagans, who do not love God; and that in this matter no one should wrong or take advantage of a brother or sister. The Lord will punish all those who commit such sins, as we told you and warned you before. For God did not call us to be impure, but to live a holy life. Therefore, anyone who rejects this instruction does not reject a human being but God, the very God who gives you his Holy Spirit. (1 Thessalonians 4:3-8)

As the above letter to the Christians in the city of Thessalonica shows, God punishes sexual sin among Christians! The ultimate punishment for sexual sin is going to hell because we are rejecting God and the Holy Spirit when we live in these sins.

It is especially bad when sexual sin is committed between Christians. The passage above states that this is taking advantage of our brothers and sisters. God has called us to live holy lives. The word "holy" means separate. We are to be separate from the world and not be conformed to its sordid patterns! Here are some Old Testament commandments about sexual purity:

Do not have sexual relations with your father's wife; that would dishonor your father.

Do not have sexual relations with your sister, either your father's daughter or your mother's daughter, whether she was born in the same home or elsewhere.

Do not have sexual relations with your son's daughter or your daughter's daughter; that would dishonor you.

Do not have sexual relations with the daughter of your father's wife, born to your father; she is your sister.

Do not have sexual relations with your father's sister; she is your father's close relative.

Do not have sexual relations with your mother's sister, because she is your mother's close relative.

Do not dishonor your father's brother by approaching his wife to have sexual relations; she is your aunt.

Do not have sexual relations with your daughter-in-law. She is your son's wife; do not have relations with her.

Do not have sexual relations with your brother's wife; that would dishonor your brother.

Do not have sexual relations with both a woman and her daughter. Do not have sexual relations with either her son's daughter or her daughter's daughter; they are her close relatives. That is wickedness.

Do not take your wife's sister as a rival wife and have sexual relations with her while your wife is living.

Do not approach a woman to have sexual relations during the uncleanness of her monthly period.

Do not have sexual relations with your neighbor's wife and defile yourself with her.

Do not give any of your children to be sacrificed to Molech, for you must not profane the name of your God. I am the Lord.

Do not have sexual relations with a man as one does with a woman; that is detestable.

Do not have sexual relations with an animal and defile yourself with it. A woman must not present herself to an animal to have sexual relations with it; that is a perversion.

Do not defile yourself in any of these ways, because this is how the nations that I am going to drive out before you *became defiled. Even the land was defiled; so I punished it for its sin, and the land vomited out its inhabitants. But you must keep my decrees and my laws. The native-born and the foreigners residing among you must not do any of these detestable things, for all these things were done by the people who lived in the land before you, and the land became defiled. And if you defile the land, it will vomit you out as it vomited out the nations that were before you. (Leviticus 18:8-28)*

God had a serious message for the Israelites. He enumerates many sexual sins that he wanted them to avoid. Why? Was it because he just wants us not to enjoy ourselves? No! God wants us to avoid sexual sin of all sorts because these types of sins have dire consequences. The nations that lived in the Promise Land before the Israelites were expelled from the land precisely because of their rampant sexual sin. Not only so, God warns the Israelites that if they commit the same sins, the same consequences would happen to them. They, too, would be occupied by the enemy! They would be expelled from the land because of their sins.

Below is some of what God has to say about sexual sins and its consequences in the New Testament:

It is God's will that you should be sanctified: that you should avoid sexual immorality; that each of you should learn to control your own body in a way that is holy and honorable, not in passionate lust like the pagans, who do not know God; and that in this matter no one should wrong or take advantage of a brother or sister. The Lord will punish all those who commit such sins, as we told you and warned you before. For God did not call us to be impure, but to live a holy life. Therefore, anyone who rejects this instruction does not reject a human being but God, the very God who gives you his Holy Spirit. (1 Thessalonians 4:3-8)

Again, we see congruency in both testaments. God says that he will punish sexual sin, and especially when we wrong our brothers and sisters in this manner. Sexual sin is serious business. The conviction we need to have is that God will punish any nation that collectively decides to live in sexual sin. He did this with the Israelites and other nations. God will also punish individuals that decide to live in this sin. This is very serious!

The progression of sexual sin has been overwhelming in the past 80 years or so in the world. For example, both my parents were born in the late 1930's and still live together as a married couple in Miami. When they were both in their 20's in the late 1950's and early 1960's, sex before marriage was something that just did not happen. According to them, the expectation was to be a virgin on one's wedding day. However, this expectation was directed mainly at women, thus showing a double standard.

Nevertheless, to not be a virgin was an embarrassment to the society. On dates, even when engaged, it was expected to have a chaperone to ensure that sexual purity was protected. No one even thought about getting divorced in those days. Adultery was rare and very hidden, as was homosexuality. These norms were a by-product of a belief in God and the Bible. "God forbid" a girl became pregnant before marriage! In those cases the mother and father were expected to marry right away as being a single mother was rare in those times.

Needless to say, society was a lot better back then in the area of purity! Things were not perfect by any means, but sexuality, for the most part, was more controlled.

How about now? Almost everybody has been very sexually impure or has had sex before marriage. Sadly, around 50% of marriages end in divorce, and many couples that are together do not get married at all.

"Currently, the cohort measure for divorce is typically calculated as being in the 40-50 percent range for couples entering their first marriage. Cohabitation: cohabiting couples have a 50-80 percent higher likelihood of divorce than non-cohabiting couples." [1]

The rate of separation in these couples is even higher. Because of this, many people do not believe in marriage anymore. Homosexuality is popular nowadays, and the media is highly sexualized in its content, tone and insinuations. Pornography is readily available for anyone to watch without any shame.

Where are we headed, sexually?

Biblically, we are headed for God's discipline! There is only so much that God is willing to take before he disciplines the nations and the world that have rampant sexual sin. That is why it is imperative that we repent of any and all sexual sin.

But how does God discipline us when we decide to live in sexual sin?

Let us consider the following passage:

> *"Therefore I have begun to destroy you,*
> *to ruin you because of your sins.*
> *You will eat and not be satisfied;*
> *your stomach will still be empty.*
> *You will store up but save nothing,*
> *because what you save, I will give to the sword.*
> *You will plant but not harvest;*
> *you will press olives but not use the oil,*
> *You will crush grapes but not drink the wine.*
> *you have observed the statutes of Omri*
> *And all the practices of Ahab's house;*
> *you have followed their traditions.*
> *Therefore I will give you over to ruin*
> *and your people to derision;*
> *you will bear the scorn of the nations." (Micah 6:13-16)*

What does God do when we live in sin? Sometimes we may think that he does nothing. But nothing could be further from the truth. Sometimes we are living in sin and nothing is appearing to happen. God sometimes does not punish sin immediately because he is giving us time to repent. (Romans 2:4) Eventually though, we cross a spiritual line and when we do, God will discipline us. But how?

The context of the passage in Micah is referring to Israel, the people of God. The equivalent today would be referring to the church, as we are God's people now. What does God tell them about living in sin?

1) You eat, but are not satisfied.
2) You store, but you do not keep.
3) You plan, but you do not reap.

What does this mean? The direct application is that God begins to destroy our lives because of our sin. Is this not the case when we decide to live in sexual sin? If we are adulterous, we can lose our spouse. We can lose our relationship with our kids. We can lose our health by getting a disease because of our immorality. We can lose our job if we "mess around" with someone at work. We can bring financial hardships on ourselves and our family if there is a separation from our spouse and children, because now we have to live somewhere else and at the same time support our family.

There is a secondary application to the passage. In time, the very sin we commit will fail to satisfy us. If we are immoral, we will not be satisfied with just one partner. We will have a *"continual lust for more."* (Ephesians 4:19) We will need additional partners. The same applies to masturbation and pornography. In time, what we indulge in will fail to satisfy. It can become an idol and lead us to leave God, yet the very idol we leave God for, will end up frustrating us and destroying us if we do not repent. This will go on until it destroys our life or until we repent. We have a choice to make!

When any of the Israelites or any foreigner residing in Israel separate themselves from me and set up idols in their hearts and put a wicked stumbling block before their faces and then go to a prophet to inquire of me, I the Lord will answer them myself. I will set my face against them and make them an example and a byword. I will remove them from my people. Then you will know that I am the Lord. (Ezekiel 14:7-8)

Any unrepentant sin becomes the idol we set up in our hearts because we come to love the sin more than God. That is precisely why we decide to practice it so much! It becomes our favorite thing to do and our place of comfort, where we go when we feel anxious or afraid. It becomes our place of rest.

Sexual sin can so easily become an idol and totally consume us. Masturbation and pornography can be idols if we do not repent of them. The same can be said for sexual immorality. We must stay away from these idols, or they will consume us and lead us to fall away from God. This is the way the enemy occupies our hearts and minds. We must fight this battle for God and gain victory!

Chapter 2
Deciding Not To Fight

We will now turn our attention to the David's first-born son, Amnon. Unfortunately, he did not imitate his father in terms of his desire to seek after God's own heart, but only in his weakness to fulfill his own sexual pleasures at the expense of others! It is interesting how often we imitate people's bad qualities rather than their good ones! Amnon decided not to fight against his lusts. Let us see what we can learn from Amnon:

> *In the course of time, Amnon son of David fell in love with Tamar, the beautiful sister of Absalom son of David. Amnon became so obsessed with his sister Tamar that he made himself ill. She was a virgin, and it seemed impossible for him to do anything to her. Now Amnon had an adviser named Jonadab son of Shimeah, David's brother. Jonadab was a very shrewd man. He asked Amnon, "Why do you, the king's son, look so haggard morning after morning? Won't you tell me?" Amnon said to him, "I'm in love with Tamar, my brother Absalom's sister." (2 Samuel 13:1-4)*

This passage is shocking! Amnon fell in "love" with his half-sister Tamar! We can get so confused as to what real love is all about. Unfortunately, this was not love but lust! It is sickening to see where the human heart can go when we are consumed by lust. Amnon was obsessed with Tamar because he could not do anything sexual with her. In addition, he was so obsessed that the fact that she was his half-sister and therefore family, meant nothing to him. He was so frustrated with his sinful desire that he literally became physically ill.

It is amazing how easily we can confuse love with lust! The world does this all the time, and as Christians, we should be on our guard as well. The question needs to be asked of single brothers and sisters in the church. In light of Amnon's lust, when we are attracted to a brother or sister, what qualities are we attracted to? Is it just the physical appearance? Spiritual qualities in a disciple need to be much more important than the physical ones! These are the qualities that we should primarily be attracted to when considering whom to select as a potential mate. We live in a world in which physical attributes are often portrayed as the most important aspect of a relationship. Unfortunately, this superficial thinking can easily seep into the church as well. We can even get so obsessed about our physical attraction to someone that, as with Amnon, it becomes all that we see. We, like Amnon, can forget that who we are attracted to are our sisters in Christ! Sexual lust can be the justification to treat them as objects for our sinful desires, rather than the precious daughters of God that they have become by God's mercy.

As previously stated, Amnon was so obsessed in his attraction to Tamar, that he became physically ill. He was consumed with this desire, and all that he wanted to do was have sex with his half-sister. There is an important principle that we can learn from this passage. The principle is:

Time does not take away sinful desires.

Sinful sexual desire does not go away with time. It can get so bad that we can get physically sick from wanting to sin sexually. The only solution is repentance. Many have fallen into masturbation or pornography or sex because they do not do something radical to repent of their lust.

We need to change our sinful desires with godly desires as the Scriptures say:

> *Those who belong to Christ Jesus have crucified the flesh with its passions and desires. (Galatians 5:24)*

> *Rather, clothe yourselves with the Lord Jesus Christ, and do not think about how to gratify the desires of the flesh. (Romans 13:14)*

> *For when we were in the realm of the flesh, the sinful passions aroused by the law were at work in us, so that we bore fruit for death. But now, by dying to what once bound us, we have been released from the law so that we serve in the new way of the Spirit, and not in the old way of the written code.*

(Romans 7:5-6)

Whoever sows to please their flesh, from the flesh will reap destruction; whoever sows to please the Spirit, from the Spirit will reap eternal life. Let us not become weary in doing good, for at the proper time we will reap a harvest if we do not give up. (Galatians 6:8-9)

We need to refuse to dwell on sinful thoughts! We need to get them out of our heads quickly by praying and reading Scriptures and by confession. If we allow ourselves to dwell on sinful thoughts, we will find a way to sin as Amnon did.

As it turns out, Amnon's cousin Jonadab devised an evil plan where Amnon pretended to be sick and have Tamar give him food in his room while both of them were alone.

Let us read 2 Samuel 13:11-19,

But when she took it to him to eat, he grabbed her and said, "Come to bed with me, my sister."

"No, my brother!" she said to him. "Don't force me! Such a thing should not be done in Israel! Don't do this wicked thing. What about me? Where could I get rid of my disgrace? And what about you? You would be like one of the wicked fools in Israel. Please

31

speak to the king; he will not keep me from being married to you." But he refused to listen to her, and since he was stronger than she, he raped her.

Then Amnon hated her with intense hatred. In fact, he hated her more than he had loved her. Amnon said to her, "Get up and get out!"

"No!" she said to him. "Sending me away would be a greater wrong than what you have already done to me."

But he refused to listen to her. He called his personal servant and said, "Get this woman out of my sight and bolt the door after her." So his servant put her out and bolted the door after her. She was wearing an ornate robe, for this was the kind of garment the virgin daughters of the king wore. Tamar put ashes on her head and tore the ornate robe she was wearing. She put her hands on her head and went away, weeping aloud as she went.

This is a very sad set of Scriptures. Because of his uncontrolled sexual desire, Amnon ended up raping his half-sister Tamar who was a virgin. After this horrific event, something perplexing happens.

Then Amnon hated her with intense hatred. In fact, he hated her more than

he had loved her. Amnon said to her,
"Get up and get out!"

His hate for Tamar after he raped her was more intense than the love that he had for her. (We know that it was not real love but lust.) From Amnon, we can glean a second principle:

Sin only satisfies while you do it.

Then, it leaves you empty. Why? Sin does not meet expectations. Once we have a deep desire to sin, it consumes us until we do it. However, when we finally do sin, it leaves us unfulfilled. Afterwards, we become addicted to feeling that feeling again, and our wickedness grows more and more. (Ephesians 4:19)

Amnon's sin did not satisfy him. He was disappointed! This will happen to us when we sin sexually. Masturbation, pornography and sexual immorality will only leave us disappointed and searching for more – Satan's trap for all men!

Solution: Only a relationship with God can truly fulfil us.

Sexual sin will not make us happy! What we think makes us happy, leaves us empty. Amnon decided not to fight against his flesh and he was miserable because of it. Let us learn from him. Only a relationship with God can truly make us happy!

Chapter 3
When We Lose The War

Unfortunately, sexual sins have consequences. Sadly, if we persist in sexual sin, there will eventually come a point in time that we will fall away from God. This does not happen right away, but nonetheless it is a warning sign for us to repent. We can and we will indeed repent! Having said that, let's look at what it means to lose the war against sexual sin!

Consider these Scriptures to take warning:

> *Saul had expelled the mediums and spiritists from the land.*
>
> *The Philistines assembled and came and set up camp at Shunem, while Saul gathered all Israel and set up camp at Gilboa. When Saul saw the Philistine army, he was afraid; terror filled his heart. He inquired of the Lord, but the Lord did not answer him by dreams or Urim or prophets. Saul then said to his attendants, "Find me a woman who is a medium, so I may go and inquire of her."*
>
> *"There is one in Endor," they said.*
>
> *So Saul disguised himself, putting on other clothes, and at night he and two*

men went to the woman. "Consult a spirit for me," he said, "and bring up for me the one I name."

But the woman said to him, "Surely you know what Saul has done. He has cut off the mediums and spiritists from the land. Why have you set a trap for my life to bring about my death?"

Then the woman asked, "Whom shall I bring up for you?"

"Bring up Samuel," he said.

When the woman saw Samuel, she cried out at the top of her voice and said to Saul, "Why have you deceived me? You are Saul!"

The king said to her, "Don't be afraid. What do you see?"

The woman said, "I see a ghostly figure coming up out of the earth."

"What does he look like?" he asked.

"An old man wearing a robe is coming up," she said.

Then Saul knew it was Samuel, and he bowed down and prostrated himself with his face to the ground.

Samuel said to Saul, "Why have you disturbed me by bringing me up?" (1 Samuel 28:3-15)

What an amazing passage! King Saul had been radical at one point and expelled the mediums and spiritists from the land. The punishment for doing this was death according to the witch of Endor. At this point in time, surely, Saul was standing for God's honor. Saul had never been to a medium!

But then he decides to drift away from God and not obey him or his prophet Samuel. In our terminology, he fell away from God!

He inquired of the Lord, but the Lord did not answer him by dreams or the Urim or by the prophets. He was far from God. He decides instead to do something terrible and go against the deep convictions he had in the past. He decides to turn to a medium to consult spirits to know about his future.

The very things he had convictions against, he decide to do. This happens to all people that fall away. When we fall away, we commit worse sins than prior to falling away from God. This is especially true when it comes to sexual sins. I have seen people who leave God sin sexually in ways that would have been incredible to them before they became Christians. Let us look at 2 Peter 2:20-21,

If they have escaped the corruption of the world by knowing our Lord and

Savior Jesus Christ and are again entangled in it and are overcome, they are worse off at the end than they were at the beginning. It would have been better for them not to have known the way of righteousness, than to have known it and then to turn their backs on the sacred command that was passed on to them.

This is intense! It is a warning for all of us. If we fall away from God, we will commit sins that we did not commit prior to becoming a Christian or they will increase in intensity.

I remember the story of a man named Manuel who was in a church that I led in Santiago, Chile. Manuel was a single brother who was not happy with his potential dating scene in the church. In the world, he had kept himself relatively pure and he was fighting to stay faithful. However, his sexual desire got the best of him, and sadly he fell away from God and went to the world. In the world, he became involved in a lot of sexual sin. About six months later, he came back to the church and wanted to get right with God. We were very happy to have him back.

Unfortunately, he had news for us. While he was enjoying his sexual sin, he had contracted HIV. Sadly, about six months later he died. I remember being at his funeral as his casket was lowered into the earth as if it was yesterday. This was the year 2001 when the treatment for HIV left much to be desired in Chile. A few weeks before he died, he told me, "Raul, I know I'm going to die. What I regret is that I will never date or marry or even lead a Bible discussion because I can't leave this hospital." In his sadness though, he was comforted as he had returned to God and had kept his faith to his dying day!

Manuel's story, sad as it is, shows us what happens when we leave God. Whatever was our sinful tendency before conversion is what we will return to when we leave God. Unfortunately, for most of us this is sexual sin. I have seen many fall away and wreck their lives with sexual sin when they leave. Even when they come back to God, the consequences of these sins follow them. This is a stern warning for us not of fall away from God. One of the reasons to stay faithful to God is to avoid the dire sexual consequences that will transpire if we decide to fall away. We need to fight with all our hearts to stay faithful to God. Even if we are falling into sexual sin in the church, we need to repent. Do not quit on God and he will not quit on us!

However, if we do fall away from God, is there hope? Can we come back after we have fallen away because of sexual sin? The answer is yes, and no. There are three categories of people who fall away or leave God and his church. In two out of three categories, the person can come back and be restored. Unfortunately, the final category of people cannot.

1. Those who were never converted.

The mind governed by the flesh is hostile to God; it does not submit to God's law, nor can it do so. Those who are in the realm of the flesh cannot please God. You, however, are not in the realm of the flesh but are in the realm of the Spirit, if indeed the Spirit of God lives in you. And if anyone does not have the Spirit of Christ, they do not belong to Christ. (Romans 8:7-9)

Paul is addressing the church in Rome in this great letter. He is talking about "Christians" who were not able to please God or submit and obey God's laws. They did not belong to Christ because they did not have the Holy Spirit! The fact that they did not have the Holy Spirit implies that they were never truly converted, even though they were part of the church. These were false Christians who "faked" their conversion just to be part of the church, and consequently, they never received the indwelling of the Holy Spirit.

Paul references false brothers and even false teachers at other points in his writings;

This matter arose because some false believers had infiltrated our ranks to spy on the freedom we have in Christ Jesus and to make us slaves. (Galatians 2:4)

I have been constantly on the move. I have been in danger from rivers, in danger from bandits, in danger from my fellow Jews, in danger from Gentiles; in danger in the city, in danger in the country, in danger at sea; and at danger from false believers. (2 Corinthians 11:26)

Peter also makes reference to false teachers in his second letter:

But there were also false prophets among the people, just as there will be false teachers among you. (2 Peter 2:1)

This is sad, but it is nonetheless a reality in the church. There will be false brothers and sister in the church from time to time. Because these people are not Christians and do not have the Holy Spirit, they cannot deny the flesh and thus continue in the same pattern of sexual sin as they were in, prior to becoming church members. They usually want to be in the church because of specific relationships they value or because they just love the friendships in general. True Christians are so loving and accepting that people want to be around them!

So technically, these church members are not fall-aways because they never were in the church in the first place. They need to come back to church and study the Bible and be properly converted. The majority of people in this category never repented of their sexual sin when they studied the Bible. Embarrassment and shame are often the reasons people lie about their sexual sin as they come closer to God. Because they do not confess this sin, they never repent of it and are never truly purified in the waters of baptism.

2. Those that wandered away.

My brothers and sisters, if one of you
should wander from the truth and
someone should bring that person
back, remember this: Whoever turns a
sinner from the error of their way will
save them from death and cover over a
multitude of sins. (James 5:19-20)

The second category of person who falls away is known
as a "wanderer." These people wander from the truth,
which implies that once they have they are not saved
anymore and must be brought back to the truth. Sadly,
they have succumbed to false doctrines. James
encourages us to bring these people back to the flock.
If these sinners repent from the error of their ways,
they will be saved from death. If they do not, they will
die. This death is a spiritual one! Once this person
repents, a multitude of their sins are covered, meaning
they are forgiven. If we fell away, then we would have
many sexual sins that would need to be covered in this
way.

3. Those who cannot come back.

It is impossible for those who have
once been enlightened, who have
tasted the heavenly gift, who have
shared in the Holy Spirit, who have
tasted the goodness of the word of God
and the powers of the coming age and
who have fallen away, to be brought
back to repentance. To their loss they

41

are crucifying the Son of God all over again and subjecting him to public disgrace. (Hebrews 6:4-6)

If we deliberately keep on sinning after we have received the knowledge of the truth, no sacrifice for sins is left, but only a fearful expectation of judgment and of raging fire that will consume the enemies of God. (Hebrews 10:26-27)

These are very strong Scriptures! God says that it is impossible for these individuals who were truly converted to come back. There is a type of a fall-away that cannot come back. These are the ones who *"deliberately"* keep on sinning after receiving knowledge of the truth. The issue here is the meaning of the word *"deliberately."* All people who leave God sin "deliberately" from a certain point of view. But there is a certain spiritual line in God's mind that if we cross it is impossible to come back to him. That is why we need to have a holy fear of him, especially when it comes down to sexual sins. This is an area where without God we can seemingly sin without limits!

For us in the church, it is basically impossible to tell if someone who wants to get restored is in the second or third category. All those who have never been truly converted can come back because they never became Christians in the first place. Because we cannot tell, we need to treat everyone as someone who can potentially come back. God will make it obvious if they can come back, as they attempt to live the Christian life once more.

Even for those who have lost the war by falling away, there is hope that they can get restored to God! Amazingly, hundreds have been restored to God after falling away. In the process, they have won the battle of sexual sin!

Part 2
The Battle Of The Heart

Chapter 4
Can We Really Overcome?

The most fundamental question we need to ask ourselves is: Can we really overcome? Can we really change our patterns of sexual impurity? Chances are, many reading this book are battling with sexual sin even as a Christian and having a hard time with feelings of defeat and shame in this area. We may even feel that we can never effect permanent change in this area of our lives. We might see temporary change, but then we eventually find ourselves falling back into impurity again and again.

This is a lie from Satan! The truth is that we can certainly change! With God and his Holy Spirit, we can change anything. The real issue is: Do we really want to change? Do we really want to put in the work it takes to change our character? If we apply the Biblical principles in this book of changing our mindset (Romans 12:1-2) through the Scriptures, we will certainly change.

Let us look at the example of someone who made perhaps one of the most radical changes in all the Scriptures, King Manasseh!

But the people did not listen. Manasseh

led them astray, so that they did more evil than the nations the Lord had destroyed before the Israelites.

The Lord said through his servants the prophets: "Manasseh king of Judah has committed these detestable sins. He has done more evil than the Amorites who preceded him and has led Judah into sin with his idols. Therefore this is what the Lord, the God of Israel, says: I am going to bring such disaster on Jerusalem and Judah that the ears of everyone who hears of it will tingle. I will stretch out over Jerusalem the measuring line used against Samaria and the plumb line use against the house of Ahab. I will wipe out Jerusalem as one wipes a dish, wiping it and turning it upside down. I will forsake the remnant of my inheritance and give them into the hands of enemies." (2 Kings 21:9-14)

Manasseh was a very bad king. As stated above, he led Judah to commit more sin than the very nations around it, nations God had them conquered and destroyed because of their sin. We see God's judgement of sin in this passage.

Manasseh's sins were numerous. In 2 Kings 21, Manasseh:

1. rebuilt the high places his father Hezekiah had

destroyed. (v.3)
2. erected altars to Baal and made Asherah poles. (v.3)
3. sacrificed his own son in the fire. (v. 6)
4. practiced divination and consulted spiritualists. (v.6)
5. put the carved Asherah pole in the Temple. (v.7)
6. shed much innocent blood in Jerusalem. (v.16)

Was there any hope for this man to repent?

The Lord spoke to Manasseh and his people, but they paid no attention. So the Lord brought against them the army commanders of the king of Assyria, who took Manasseh prisoner, put a hook in his nose, bound him with bronze shackles, and took him to Babylon. In his distress he sought the favor of the Lord his God and humbled himself greatly before the God of his ancestors. And when he prayed to him, the Lord was moved by his entreaty and listened to his plea; so he brought him back to Jerusalem and to his kingdom. Then Manasseh knew that the Lord is God. (2 Chronicles 33:10-13)

The Lord's discipline came upon Manasseh because of his sin. He was taken to Babylon, reduced from king to a mere slave with a hook in his nose and bound with bronze shackles. It was there in Babylon in the midst of suffering that he decided to pray to God and seek forgiveness. God amazingly heard his prayer and brought him back to Jerusalem!

Back in Jerusalem, he took steps to prove his repentance by his deeds, as seen in 2 Chronicles 33. Manasseh:

1. rebuilt the outer wall of the city of David. (v. 14)
2. got rid of the foreign gods. (v. 15)
3. removed the image from the Temple of the Lord. (v. 15)
4. removed all the altars he had built. (v. 15)
5. restored the altar of the Lord and the offerings. (v. 16)

This amazing account gives us the answer to our question: Can we change? The answer is a resounding YES! Manasseh changed! He repented so radically, it is nearly unbelievable.

What is the lesson? If Manasseh changed, we can definitely change as well. There is no sin of which we cannot repent. We need to have a basic conviction that anyone, including ourselves, can change. Oftentimes, the hardest person to convince we CAN change is ourselves. We can and must change to please God with our lives. Only if we believe we can change, will all the practicals that are later described in this book help us. If we do not believe we can change, there are no practicals, programs or people that can help us. Accountability – though helpful – never replaces faith in God's ability to help us. It all boils down to our faith.

How can we get the faith to believe we can change?

Now faith is confidence in what we hope for and assurance about what we do not see. This is what the ancients were commended for. (Hebrews 11:1)

The basic definition of faith is quite simple: It is believing in what we do not see and seeing something before it happens. We *"see"* what we want in our mind and we believe it can happen.

Faith is a basic law for our spiritual existence on earth. God blesses faith even if we are not a Christian. For example, when we start university, we do not think; "Well, I will study for three years, and then I will drop out." All the work we put in and all the studying, just for nothing? Would any of us be willing to go into major debt because of the student loans we take out to study for a degree knowing that we will not finish? Imagine thinking like that!

Another example is when we get married. Our spouse is the person we love most, and therefore, we are fired up when we get married. We do not get married thinking, "I will marry this woman and after ten years and two children, we will get a divorce." That would be ludicrous. When we get married, we believe we are marrying the person whom we will spend the rest of our lives.

These two examples show us the issue of faith. Everything we do has to do with faith at some level. Yet, interestingly enough, when it comes down to having faith we can change for God, we often falter. However, faith is precisely what we need in order to finally be pure. The question becomes: How can I be pure when I have so many defeats in this area? This is a good question. The way to answer this question is to understand more about the basic nature of faith.

A very strong Scripture is: 1 Thessalonians 4:3-7,

> *It is God's will that you should be sanctified: that you should avoid sexual immorality; that each of you should learn to control your own body in a way that is holy and honorable, not in passionate lust like the pagans, who do not know God; and that in this matter no one should wrong or take advantage of a brother or sister. The Lord will punish all those who commit such sins, as we told you and warned you before. For God did not call us to be impure, but to live a holy life.*

From this passage and many others, it becomes obvious that God wants us to be pure sexually. Because we know this, we can now combine this passage with 1 John 5:14-15,

> *This is the confidence we have in approaching God: that if we ask anything according to his will, he hears us. And if we know that he hears us – whatever we ask – we know that we have what we asked of him.*

This passage states that there is a confidence we can have when we approach God in prayer. If we pray anything according to his will, he will hear us and answer. Now, we know from 1 Thessalonians 4:3-7 that God wants us to pray for our purity. That means he wants to answer this very specific prayer. What do we need next? James 1:6-8 has the answer:

> *But when you ask, you must believe and not doubt, because the one who doubts is like a wave of the sea, blown and tossed by the wind. That person should not expect to receive anything from the Lord. Such a person is double-minded and unstable in all they do.*

This is the next step. We must believe our prayer about being pure. If we just believe, God will grant us the purity! Why? He will answer because we are praying something in accordance with his will. All we need to do is believe and God will answer our prayer.

It is important to understand that we need to believe even before we pray. We can wrestle with God in prayer, but we need to fundamentally believe before we pray.

In conclusion, we have seen in this chapter that we can indeed overcome. God wants us to overcome. We have the tools to overcome with God. We also have the tools to overcome with other Christians helping us in this battle. The question then becomes: Do you want to overcome? Let us overcome and give glory to God!

Chapter 5
Seeing The Potential To Win

Once we have the faith to believe we can change, we need to embrace the truth about sexual sin. Sadly, it is easy to get used to thinking that sexual sin is acceptable. This is twisted thinking. Impurity and sexual sins are symptoms of something deeper. They are symptoms of not understanding the truth. In John 8:31-32, the Bible states:

> *To the Jews who had believed him, Jesus said, "If you hold to my teaching, you are really my disciples. Then you will know the truth, and the truth will set you free."*

If we are not set free from sin, it means we do not know the truth. In this passage, we see five consecutive steps we need to follow to set ourselves free. They are: 1) believe, 2) obey, 3) be a disciple, 4) know the truth, and 5) be set free.

In John 8:34, the Bible tells us what we are being set free from:

> *Jesus replied, "Very truly I tell you, everyone who sins is a slave to sin."*

To be set free from sin, we have to know the truth. To know the truth, we need to be a disciple of Jesus. In order to be a disciple of Jesus, we need to continue to obey him by holding on to his teachings. And to obey his teachings, we first have to have faith in Jesus and believe in him.

When we do not obey God by being involved in sexual sin, our view of the truth gets blurry and twisted. It is impossible to know the truth of God while living in sexual sin. Titus 1:15 reads:

> *To the pure, all things are pure, but to those who are corrupted and do not believe, nothing is pure.*

This is deep! We see life according to the righteousness of our hearts! That is why sexual sin is a symptom of having an impure heart. Sexually impure people see life from a twisted point of view. They do not know the truth of God. It goes even further:

> *To the faithful you show yourself faithful,*
> *to the blameless you show yourself blameless,*
> *To the pure you show yourself pure,*
> *but to the devious you show yourself shrewd.*
> *You save the humble*
> *but bring low those whose eyes are haughty. (Psalm 18:25-27)*

This passage teaches that we see God according to our righteousness. When we are impure or in sin in general, it skews our personal view of God. If we are faithful, we see God as faithful. If we are pure, we see

God as pure. If we are devious, we see God as shrewd. That means that we see God as playing a cruel joke on us. We do not see God as a loving, sovereign God who permits everything for our ultimate good. (Romans 8:28) In other words, we do not see the truth about who God is.

Sexual impurity is a symptom that there is a lot going wrong spiritually inside of us, aside from the obvious sexual sin. Sometimes, we want to compartmentalize our sin. We may say things like, "My only weakness is impurity, but in the other areas, I'm doing good." That is not true! Our whole spirituality is connected. People who are impure are usually bitter in areas of their lives, or full of pride, not wanting to submit to God. People who are impure are full of selfishness, and do not have a faith in the power of God working in their ministry. Lying is also a part of impurity because we want to hide the truth because of possible embarrassment before other Christians. Impurity also affects our relationships because we become self-conscious. It makes us live in a constant state of guilt, which for some robs them of their faith and of the ability to form and sustain good relationships. In essence, we create our own version of God's truth, which is in fact a lie.

How can we know the truth again and have a pure heart? Revelation 2:4-5 reads:

> *Yet I hold this against you: You have forsaken the love you had at first. Consider how far you have fallen! Repent and do the things you did at first. If you do not repent, I will come*

to you and remove your lampstand from its place.

There are no shortcuts! We have to put the time and effort into working on our relationship with God. We need to remember how far we have fallen when we become impure or commit sexual sin. We have to remember where we were at one point with God – how when we were young Christians, we were above all grateful for our salvation!

It is therefore imperative that we renew our gratitude for the cross of Jesus, for the fact that Jesus died for our sins. It also means being grateful for the life God originally spared us from before we were Christians.

For Christ's love compels us, because we are convinced that one died for all, and therefore all died. And he died for all, that those who live should no longer live for themselves but for him who died for them and was raised again. (2 Corinthians 5:14-15)

It is Christ's love that compels us and motivates us to change. We need to remember the awesome life God gave us when we were baptized, and it will motivate us to be pure. This is remembering the height from which we have fallen. We do this by doing the things we used to do at first when we were young Christians. When we were young Christians we were eager to do great things. What were the things we did at first?

1) Daily Prayer

During the days of Jesus's life on earth, he offered up prayers and petitions with fervent cries and tears to the one who could save him from death, and he was heard because of his reverent submission. (Hebrews 5:7)

If Jesus had to pray with loud cries and tears, how much more do we need to pray? Our prayer life is of paramount importance to helping us regain our first love and cleanse us from sexual sin!

It is very important to have daily prayers in which we connect with God. It is a great privilege that we have, to connect with the Creator of the universe, and it is one of the main ways to recover our first love for God and stay pure.

We fail because we fail to pray! We need to pray because we love God and want to be close to him. Being close to God is precisely what is going to keep us pure.

2) Daily Bible Study

Jesus answered, "It is written: 'Man shall not live on bread alone, but on every word that comes from the mouth of God." (Matthew 4:4)

If we do not eat physically, we eventually get sick. If we do not eat for a prolonged period of time, we eventually die. It is the same with us spiritually. We need to eat spiritually (read the Bible) in order to prevent getting sick spiritually and eventually dying, which is the same as falling away from God.

Young Christians are in awe of the Scriptures that changed their lives! The Bible is a novelty to them. They are fired up about what they are learning in the word of God. When we are coming back to God, we need to have the same attitude towards our personal Bible study. We need to fall in love with the word of God. This means that we read the word with the expectation that God will always teach us something when we read it.

I have been a Christian for twenty years, and the Bible is as new to me now as it was twenty years ago. The issue is our mindset. The word of God is spiritual. It is always teaching us if we have the heart to be taught. When we start learning again from the word of God, our purity will increase in dramatic measures!

3) Daily Evangelism

> *For when I preach the gospel, I cannot boast, since I am compelled to preach. Woe to me if I do not preach the gospel! If I preach voluntarily, I have a reward; if not voluntarily, I am simply discharging the trust committed to me. (1 Corinthians 9:16-17)*

One of the first things that we lose when we lose our first love is our desire to preach the word. We stop being fishers of men! Evangelism is not an activity of the church. It is the identity of every true Christian!

Evangelism not only saves people, it keeps us saved as well, because we are constantly reminding ourselves of the many things we have in Christ. (Philemon 6) If we have the cure for the spiritual cancer of the world, which is sin, how can we dare not share it? This would be horrific selfishness!

Let us make a decision to share our faith every day and thus fulfil our God-given purpose of making disciples of all nations. When we are busy seeking and saving the lost, we do not have time to sin sexually. Following Jesus in this way will keep us pure!

4) Daily Discipling

> **See to it, brothers and sisters, that none of you has a sinful, unbelieving heart that turns away from the living God. But encourage one another daily, as long as it is called "Today," so that none of you may be hardened by sin's deceitfulness. (Hebrews 3:12-13)**

We all sin. Sin hardens and deceives the human heart. This is what happens when we lose our first love. The antidote is in this Scripture. We all need daily encouragement from other brothers and sisters so that our hearts do not get deceived and hardened. This is discipling! It is having someone in your life who will be a spiritual mentor helping you spiritually.

God says we all need this in our lives. This special brother or sister can help keep us accountable in the area of sexual temptation. We can confess our sins to him or her (James 5:16) and have a great friend of the same sex who will help us spiritually. Discipling relationships keep us on the "straight and narrow," and help us stay pure in this dark world.

5) Daily Humility

The sins of Sodom and Gomorrah were atrocious! Unfortunately, they are infamous in the Scriptures. What sins are these two cities known for?

> *Before they had gone to bed, all the men from every part of the city of Sodom – both young and old – surrounded the house. They called to Lot, "Where are the men who came to you tonight? Bring them out to us so that we can have sex with them." (Genesis 19:4-5)*

This has to be one of the most shocking Scriptures in the whole Bible! It says that all the men of Sodom surrounded the house. Both young and old surrounded it. These men's lust had no bounds. They wanted to have sex with Lot's two visitors and rape these two men. They wanted to have homosexual sex with these men without their consent. Unbeknownst to them, these two men happened to be angels!

The story of Sodom and Gomorrah illustrates that if we do not control sexual sin, it can totally consume us. Surely, the men who surrounded the house could have had sex with each other, and they surely did many times. But they wanted new flesh. They were not satisfied in their own homosexual sin with each other.

> *The eye never has enough of seeing,*
> *Nor the ear its fill of hearing.*
> *(Ecclesiastes 1:8)*

But why? What is the root of Sodom's sin? The Scriptures tell us:

> **Now this was the sin of your sister Sodom: She and her daughters were arrogant, overfed and unconcerned; they did not help the poor and needy. They were haughty and did detestable things before me. Therefore, I did away with them as you have seen. (Ezekiel 16:49-50)**

The prophet Ezekiel, many years later, tells us what the root of Sodom's sin was – arrogance! Pride led them to be overfed and unconcerned. Afterwards, they did detestable things before the Lord, including the gross homosexuality they practiced.

The principle we see here is: Arrogance or pride preceded sexual sin. Pride is a sense of independence from God and God's people. Basically, when we are full of pride, we put God out of the picture and decide to do what we want. Foolishly enough, we think that we will not suffer any consequences. As our own person, we feel entitled to do things our own way, and that no one has the right to tell us what to do. We are, dare we say, the "god" of our own lives.

Satan himself fell because of his pride! Let us look at Isaiah 14:12-15,

> *How you have fallen from heaven,*
> *Morning star, son of the dawn!*
> *You have been cast down to the earth,*
> *You who once laid low the nations!*
> *You said in your heart,*
> *"I will ascend to the heavens;*
> *I will raise my throne*
> *Above the stars of God;*
> *I will sit enthroned on the mount of assembly,*
> *On the utmost heights of Mount Zaphon.*
> *I will ascend above the tops of the clouds;*
> *I will make myself like the Most High."*
> *But you are brought down to the realm of the dead,*
> *To the depths of the pit.*

Satan himself was cast out of heaven because he wanted to be on God's throne. He basically wanted to be God! This is the root of all pride. Impure people are prideful because they want to control their lives. They give themselves a license to do what they ought not to do, because they think they are in control of their lives. For example, they masturbate and watch pornography because they do not believe God can give them the self-control they need. For them the feeling seems too strong to deny. They are immoral, because they do not believe God has an awesome spouse waiting for them in the future, nor are they willing to develop the character to wait for God's provision in their life. They also do not believe that there will be consequences for their actions. Once we decide to be independent of God, it is only a matter of time until we cater to our own sensual and sexual desires.

We need to be humble in order to be pure for our God. Humility is the opposite of pride! It is a sense of dependence on God and interdependence with God's people. God is good and wants to bless us with self-control and with a spouse for the majority of people, but we need to be humble and trust our loving and awesome God.

The only way to purity is by being humble.

> *The way of fools seems right to them,*
> *But the wise listen to advice. (Proverbs*
> *12:15)*

The fool thinks he is always right, which is obvious pride. The proud do not listen to advice. We have got to listen to advice in the area of sexual purity. This is an area we need lots of advice in because most of us have damaged ourselves in this area.

> *Listen to advice and accept discipline,*
> *And at the end you will be counted*
> *among the wise. (Proverbs 19:20)*

We need to impose on ourselves parameters in order to stay pure. We should discuss these parameters with other disciples to help us stay accountable too.

Parameters are self-imposed rules that we abide by to protect ourselves and others from falling into sexual sin. Please see the chapter on dating to find some good examples!

We may say that parameters can be extreme and that we do not need them, that we can perfectly control ourselves. We may believe we have the strength to control ourselves sensually and sexually, but we forget one thing: Our brothers and sisters. Perhaps they do not have the self-control we have. It is selfish to just think in terms of what benefits our sense of pride and independence and not to think about others and their weaknesses.

Besides, no one is strong according to the word of God. We may have success in our purity ten times in a row, even if we do something unwise but then fall the eleventh time because we decided to trust in ourselves. This is why Scripture says:

> *So, if you think you are standing firm, be careful that you don't fall! (1 Corinthians 10:12)*

Not only do we need help given to us, we need to be humble enough to seek out help on our own accord and love the correction we receive from others who love us and use the word of God.

> *Let a righteous man strike me – that is a kindness;*
> *Let him rebuke me – that is oil on my head.*

My head will not refuse it. *(Psalm 141:5)*

We need to love being corrected and rebuked by righteous men and women, because these rebukes will save us from making decisions that can lead us to fall into sexual sin.

Here is some advice about personal purity that I have found wise and useful regarding times when we feel more tempted to be impure or immoral:

1) <u>Test week</u>: If we are students and have tests, it is very stressful and some look for impurity to find comfort.

2) <u>Disappointment and problems</u>: When we are going through a hard time, we need comfort. This is when we need to seek God the most, but it is easy to turn to sensuality or sex instead.

3) <u>Early morning</u>: Most young men wake up aroused, and this is a time of temptation. Seek God early in the morning every day through prayer and Bible study to avoid temptation at this time. Get out of bed right away – practice the Stop (the alarm clock) - Drop (immediately to your knees next to your bed) - and Pray method!

4) <u>Late night</u>: Late at night we are tired because of all we have done during the day. Most have a tendency to drop their spiritual guard at this time and sexual thoughts can come easily. Be aware of this time of temptation and read the Bible or pray and

listen to spiritual music. Fellowship can be helpful as well.

5) Holidays: Although we have more time, our tendency is to take a vacation from God, which is why many fall into sin during this time. The solution is to have a spiritual plan for the holidays before you leave.

6) Shower: It goes without saying that the temptation arises here because we are naked, alone and there is water. Be aware of this time and make the decision to pray before all showers and never touch ourselves in any inappropriate way.

7) Being alone/naps: Being alone can be a dangerous time for a disciple of Jesus because our minds tend to wander. Many times that wandering can lead to impure thoughts, which in turn can lead to impurity and immorality. We need to be aware of this and try to be about the Lord's business of seeking and saving the lost or in fellowship with disciples and not be idle. We need to minimize the time we are alone. If we have to study, try to do it in a public place like a university library or a coffee shop.

These are some of the things that can trigger intense sexual temptation. Let us be aware, be humble to take advice and have great victories for God.

In conclusion, when we are in sexual sin, there is a lot more going wrong with us than just the sexual sin itself. Sexual sin deceives us from knowing God's truth. The truth gets twisted in our lives. The only solution is to gain back our first love and do the things we did at first. Once we have gone back to our first love, our relationship with God will be awesome! The consequence of this will be sexual purity. Like the Scripture says:

Blessed are the pure in heart,
For they will see God. (Matthew 5:8)

Chapter 6
Motivation To Fight

What motivates us to fight for our sexual purity? There are five basic motivations for us to change found in the Bible:

1. Pain (or discipline)
2. Love
3. Grace
4. Rewards (in this case heaven)
5. Fear of God

We will look at the first four of these key motivators in this chapter and the fifth in the following chapter. To understand the first motivation, pain or discipline, let us first look to the fourth son of Jacob – Judah.

Judah was one of Jacob's twelve sons. This is not the tribe of Judah that came from his lineage. This was the patriarch Judah, the brother of Joseph. He was one of the ten brothers who wanted to kill Joseph because of their father's favoritism towards him and because of his dreams, which put him above his brothers.

But they saw him in the distance, and before he reached them, they plotted to kill him.

> *"Here comes that dreamer!" they said to each other. "Come now, let's kill him and throw him into one of these cisterns and say that a ferocious animal devoured him. Then we'll see*

what comes of his dreams." (Genesis 37:18-20)

It was Judah himself who came up with the idea to sell his brother to the Ishmaelites rather than kill him. We can see this in Genesis 37:26-27,

Judah said to his brothers, "What will we gain if we kill our brother and cover up his blood? Come, let's sell him to the Ishmaelites and not lay our hands on him; after all, he is our brother, our own flesh and blood." His brothers agreed.

Judah did not desire to have Joseph killed, but he still did something very horrible in having Joseph sold as a slave! The pain and suffering that Joseph went through because of this was atrocious, and it goes without saying about the pain he caused his father Jacob, as Joseph was indeed his favorite son. At the end of the day, Judah was selfish. He was only thinking about himself and his pain and the injustice committed against him.

Judah was also an immoral man. When his widowed daughter-in-law pretended to be a prostitute by the side of the road, he did not hesitate at all to have sex with her. The details of this are in Genesis 38. Judah's immorality was indicative that there was a lot wrong with him spiritually. Judah's moral and spiritual character was far from God's!

We now fast-forward many years later when Joseph

finally becomes the administrator of all of Egypt and the right hand of Pharaoh. There is now a great famine in the land, so much so that Jacob's sons had to go to Egypt to buy food. It is noteworthy that Joseph had a little brother named Benjamin who was his only full brother. Jacob's affection towards Benjamin was as deep as it had been towards Joseph.

At this time, Joseph was questioning his brothers and had not revealed to them that he was indeed their brother. Joseph had the idea of keeping Benjamin with him as a prisoner until his father came. Now here we see the change in Judah's heart. He says in Genesis 44:30-34,

> *So now, if the boy is not with us when I go back to your servant my father, and if my father, whose life is closely bound up with the boy's life, sees that the boy isn't there, he will die. Your servants will bring the gray head of our father down to the grave in sorrow. Your servant guaranteed the boy's safety to my father. I said, "If I do not bring him back to you, I will bear the blame before you, my father, all my life!*

> *"Now then, please let your servant remain here as my lord's slave in place of the boy, and let the boy return with his brothers. How can I go back to my father if the boy is not with me? No! Do not let me see the misery that would come on my father."*

We now see a changed Judah! How did he change and go from selling his own brother Joseph to being willing to sacrifice his life for his little brother Benjamin? Pain is the answer. **He did not want his father to suffer more pain by losing another one of his sons. He loved his father. As we see, we can only change when we associate our sin with causing pain to those you love and care about.** This is precisely how Judah repented. His father, Jacob, still had favoritism towards Benjamin, but that was not the issue anymore. Judah loved his father deeply and did not want to see him in pain. He had already hurt him enough by selling Joseph to Egypt and had undoubtedly seen the effect on his father for many years.

How does this relate to repenting from sexual sin? It relates perfectly. How can we stop masturbating and watching pornography? How can we stop being sexually immoral? Pain! When we sin sexually, we hurt those we love. We hurt our spouse. We hurt our girlfriend or boyfriend. We hurt our parents. We hurt our brothers and sisters in the church. We ultimately hurt God. We hurt our father in heaven, whom we have already hurt enough when we caused Jesus to die on the cross for our sins. What is more important, a few seconds of pleasure or living with the pain that we cause those we love?

We need to associate our sexual sin with hurting our loved ones including our God. This is an awesome motivation to help us to change!

Another man who changed was Jacob, Judah's father.

His change was motivated by his love for God – our second motivation.

> *So Jacob was left alone, and a man wrestled with him till daybreak. When the man saw that he could not overpower him, he touched the socket of Jacob's hip so that his hip was wrenched as he wrestled with the man. Then the man said, "Let me go, for it is daybreak."*
>
> *But Jacob replied, "I will not let you go unless you bless me."*
>
> *The man asked him, "What is your name?"*
>
> *"Jacob," he answered.*
>
> *Then the man said, "Your name will no longer be Jacob, but Israel, because you have struggled with God and with humans and have overcome." (Genesis 32:24-28)*

This is an incredible account of how Jacob changed! He changed so much that God decided to change his name. The name Jacob means "grasps his heel," which is a Hebrew idiom for "he deceives." The name Israel means "he who wrestles with God."

The lesson of Jacob was a simple one: Perseverance! He wrestled with God until he was blessed. What were the blessings that he was seeking? His estranged brother Esau, whom he had not seen in many years, was coming to meet him along with 400 of his men. Jacob thought Esau wanted to kill him because Jacob had stolen his birthright and father's blessing earlier, which led to Jacob fleeing many years before. Jacob saw his impending doom coming with Esau. He was totally alone with his God.

He really wanted to save his family from certain death because he loved his family. This is why the angel came to test him. God tested Jacob's resolve through the angel. The angel wrestled with Jacob the entire night and even injured him, but Jacob would not stop fighting! He would not stop fighting until his situation changed.

Jacob passed the test. God gave him the blessing he was desiring. God changed Esau's heart and instead of killing him, they hugged and cried together when they met. His family was now saved! God gave him a great victory!

We need Jacob's heart and resolve in order to be pure. We need to persevere with God in prayer until he changes us. We need to wrestle with God until he blesses us with purity. We often do not persevere long enough to see true change, and consequently, we remain in a cycle of impurity because we are not like Jacob. Jacob understood that he needed to save his family from death because he loved them. He did not want to lose his family whom he loved so much.

Jacob was desperate! Herein lies our problem. We are

often not desperate enough to change. We are not like Jacob who saw the approaching danger to him and his family. Sexual sin will eventually kill all who practice it. We can lose everything because of it. We need to be desperate to change in this area. We also need to be desperate to be pure because we do not want to hurt God. God is the person we need to love the most. We also do not want to hurt our spouses, children and church family. We need to be desperate because of love.

Love is very much connected to our next motivation – grace. Grace is receiving a gift we do not deserve. As Christians, we have received the forgiveness of sins through Jesus Christ. We do not deserve this. Because of Christ's great gift to us, we decide to live a life of gratitude, and we thus deny ourselves the desires of the flesh because we love our God who gave us grace!

For the grace of God has appeared that offers salvation to all people. It teaches us to say, "No" to ungodliness and worldly passions, and to live self-controlled, upright and godly lives in this present age, while we wait for the blessed hope – the appearing of the glory of our great God and Savior, Jesus Christ. (Titus 2:11-13)

The grace of God is absolutely necessary to be able to overcome sexual sin. The passage above teaches us one basic thing about the relationship between sin and grace: It teaches us to say "no" to sin. The problem is that often we say "yes" to sin. The grace of God does the opposite. How does it teach us to say "no?" Grace is receiving what we do not deserve. We deserve to go to hell for our sins. But God showed us grace by sending Jesus to die for us. We can be disciples today and be forgiven of our sins because Jesus has given us what we do not deserve. Why do we become disciples in the first place? God's grace! Why do we remain disciples? The same!

We remain disciples because we are grateful. We are grateful that we are saved and going to heaven one day. This gratitude is what teaches us to say "no" to sin. We do not want to sin because we do not want to hurt God anymore. Gratitude is the only motivation that will keep us faithful in the long run. Gratitude is the best motivation in the world to remain faithful and to be pure for our God.

The passage in Titus also teaches us about one of the most underutilized motivations for staying pure – heaven! This happens to be a motivation that often eludes us. Many Christians do not think about heaven enough. We get so caught up with doing things here in this world that we forget where we are going. It is very important to read the Bible, pray and evangelize every day. It is imperative that we are in Bible studies with our non-Christian friends so that they become disciples. But why do we do all this? Obviously, we do all this because we want them to be saved and to have a relationship with God like we do. But why do we want them to have a relationship with God and be saved? We want this because we want them to make it to heaven one day.

Heaven is the ultimate motivation. Being with God one day is what everything is about. Some of us may be more consumed with what we do than where we are going. That is why many once-committed disciples "burn out." In this number includes not a few Christian leaders.

The grace of God teaches us to wait for the *"blessed hope,"* that is to wait for Jesus. If our hope is not in Jesus and in being with him one day, we will not understand the grace of God. Besides, if we do not want to be with God here on earth, why would God want you to be with him in heaven?

> *Dear friends, now we are children of God, and what we will be has not yet been made known. But we know that when Christ appears, we shall be like him, for we shall see him as he is. All who have this hope in him purify themselves, just as he is pure. (1 John 3:2-3)*

Having a hope of being with Jesus in heaven purifies our minds. We do not want to sin sexually because we do not want to "mess up" our chances of going to heaven.

Chapter 7
Delight In The Fear Of The Lord

Although the grace and love of God are deep motivations for us to remain pure, there is one additional motivation that we must discuss in more detail. This is the fear of God. Often times, the fear of God is something misunderstood. This error, in part, lies in the fact that we try not to fear anything. To fear something or someone is often seen as a weakness. Many who profess to follow Jesus just want to love God and not fear him because we see God as a loving God and not as someone who is eager to discipline us when we do something wrong! This is not a complete view of who God is. His discipline is actually a facet of his love!

How wrong our view of God can be at times! If we do not fear God, we cannot possibly be pure or make it to heaven. Fearing God is of primary importance to be saved and to make it to heaven one day.

What is the best definition of the fear of the Lord? In Luke 12:4-5 Jesus says,

> *I tell you, my friends, do not be afraid of those who kill the body and after that can do no more. But I will show you whom you should fear: Fear him who, after your body has been killed, has authority to throw you into hell. Yes, I tell you, fear him.*

Jesus says not to fear men because the worst they can do to you is kill you. He goes on further to say that we need to fear God because he can not only kill you but throw you into hell. We know that to be in hell is to be eternally separated from God! There is no relationship with God if we are in hell. Therefore, the definition of fearing God in this passage is the fear of losing our relationship with him!

This is deep! If we see the fear of God like this, it will most certainly help us be pure. For example, one of the reasons a husband does not want to cheat on his wife is because if he does, he can lose the relationship with her by a divorce. So, the fear of losing his relationship with his wife helps him not be adulterous. The same principle can be applied to God. Why try with all our heart, mind, soul and strength to be pure? Because if we do not, we can eventually lose our relationship with God.

Let us look at three principles about the fear of the Lord and how they can help with our purity.

1) The fear of the Lord is pure, enduring forever. (Psalm 19:9)

The fear of the Lord is not something bad. It is something good and pure. It is a respect and an admiration. It is something we need to keep us faithful. There is a saying, "If the love of the Lord does not motivate you, let at least the fear of him do so." In other words, if the love of God does not motivate you, then at least let your fear of him be your motivation to start.

The whole point is to obey God and be pure.

For example, I fear putting my finger into the electric socket. This is actually a good fear. If I were to do that, I would be shocked – literally! I would also be a fool. It is good to have a healthy fear of electricity because it is a stronger power than us. It does not mean that we go around all day worried and depressed about the possibility of being shocked. Nor do we go around having bitterness and bad attitudes towards electricity. We just make the decision not to put our finger in the electric socket. I dare say that we generally have a great relationship with electricity!

With God, it is somewhat similar. We need a healthy fear of God in order not to fall into sexual sin. Let us look at a Scripture in Isaiah about Jesus in reference to the fear of the Lord:

> *A shoot will come up from the stump of Jesse;*
> *From his roots a Branch will bear fruit.*
> *The Spirit of the Lord will rest on him – the Spirit of wisdom and of understanding, the Spirit of counsel and of might, the Spirit of the knowledge and fear of the Lord – and he will delight in the fear of the Lord. (Isaiah 11:1-3)*

The above passage is a prophecy about Jesus and how he would be full of the Spirit. It states that Jesus delighted in the fear of the Lord! To delight in something is to deeply enjoy it. I delight sometimes in having a good meal! I particularly like sushi! So, my wife and I plan for it. We are fired up in our anticipation of that meal. Once it comes, we delight in it. We enjoy a sushi meal with our whole heart!

In a similar way, Jesus delighted in the fear of the Lord! If our Lord and Savior delighted in the fear of the Lord, how much more should we? Just like the fear of the Lord is pure, we can take it a step further and delight in it. We delight in him by understanding that God wants us to fear him for our own good! The fear of the Lord saves us from death. We can delight in his marvelous plan of creating this necessity of us fearing him. We can delight in his genius!

He knows we are like children sometimes and very prone to abusing his goodness. He knows that when everything is going well, we would most likely take advantage of his goodness and not follow him. We really are like spoiled children when it comes to him. That is why we can delight in Him and in His plan. God is awesome. We need to thank him for the fear of the Lord. We would not stay faithful without it. Let us change our mindset about how we view the fear of the Lord, and let us enjoy the great benefits of it and be pure.

2) **We cannot love God without fearing him and we cannot fear him without loving him.**

And now, Israel, what does the Lord your God ask of you but to Fear the Lord your God, to walk in obedience to

him, to love him, to serve the Lord your
God with all your heart and with all
your soul, and to observe the Lord's
commands and decrees that I am
giving you today for your own good.
(Deuteronomy 10:12-13)

When Jesus is asked the most important
commandment, he sad in Matthew 22:37, *"Love the*
Lord your God with all your heart and with all your
soul and with all your mind." Without a doubt, Jesus
is quoting from Deuteronomy. In the Scripture above,
we can glean a great insight into the fear of the Lord.

The above Deuteronomy passage goes on to ask a
question: "What does the Lord your God ask of you?"
This is a great question. Everyone wants to know what
God expects from us. The first thing God says is that he
wants us to fear him, because if we fear God, we will
obey him. Then it says that God wants us to love him
with all our being. It seems that fearing God is a
precondition to loving him. It is part of loving him.
From this passage we can glean this principle: We
cannot love God without fearing him, and we cannot
fear God without loving him!

We cannot have one without the other. The two are
"two sides of the same coin." One of the reasons many
who call themselves Christians do not love God is that
they do not fear him. Their lack of a holy fear does not
lead them to obey God and thus stay pure. Many of us
do not fear God, and thus are in perpetual impurity
because we do not understand the fear of God. Others
might be unknowingly fearing God because we just

have a heart simply to obey him and thus stay pure. Those of us with this gift from God of purity of heart need to be aware of Satan's schemes: To take away our fear of God and thus make us vulnerable once again to the sexual temptations! This is why bitterness for older brothers is so dangerous because a sense of entitlement or complaining spirit can rob us of fear of God leaving us vulnerable to Satan's attacks!

3) The fear of the Lord takes away all our other fears.

As humans we have a tendency to fear everything except God. We fear losing our jobs. We fear being stuck in a traffic jam. We have fears about our financial situation and where that could lead us. We fear solitude and not being able to make good friendships or having a "special someone." We fear our children's future. Most of us definitely fear failure. We fear possible health issues in ourselves and in our families. We fear death as we get older. The truth is simple: We live in fear of everything! We tend to fear everything in our lives except God!

All of these things, put incredible pressure in our lives. Our flesh cries out for a little bit of relief. Thus enters sexual sin! Sexual sin gives us a momentary relief of all the pressures of our lives. The problem is that it is just that – a momentary relief. Through our relationship with God, we can have not just a momentary relief from our pressures and burdens, but a permanent relief that comes from the Holy Spirit as he daily empowers us to handle any and all pressures.

If someone were to say that we could eliminate of all our fears and that this will in turn keep us pure and away from sexual sin, we would most likely not believe the person. Yet this is exactly what the Scriptures teach in Luke 12:4-7,

> *I tell you, my friends, do not be afraid of those who kill the body and after that can do no more. But I will show you whom you should fear: Fear him who, after your body has been killed, has authority to throw you into hell. Yes, I tell you, fear him. Are not five sparrows sold for two pennies? Yet not one of them is forgotten by God. Indeed, the very hairs of your head are all numbered. Don't be afraid; you are worth more than many sparrows.*

We have seen this Scripture already, but here the extra verses complete the thought. Obviously we need to fear God and not men. But the last verses are so encouraging. God cares about even sparrows. Sparrows are not forgotten by God. He cares about them and meets their needs. How much more does God care about us as humans that are made in his image? Of course, he will care about us. That is why Jesus says, *"Don't be afraid; you are worth more than many sparrows."*

What is Jesus trying to say? It seems somewhat confusing that we have to fear God but do not need to be afraid in the end. What Jesus is saying is that when we fear God and only him, he will take care of us, like as he does with the sparrows. Therefore, we do not have to fear anything else in life!

The fear of God takes away all fears!

Psalm 112:6-8 reads:

> *Surely the righteous will never be shaken;*
> *They will be remembered forever.*
> *They will have no fear of bad news;*
> *Their hearts are steadfast, trusting in the Lord.*
> *Their hearts are secure, they will have no fear;*
> *In the end they will look in triumph on their foes.*

God is an expert in taking away our fears. He is only going to do that when we are striving for righteousness as the passage above dictates.

When we do not fear life in general, we are not stressed. We are close to God and constantly pray and meditate on his word. We are at peace, and thus we have no need to turn to masturbation or pornography or sexual immorality because we are living in perfect peace and harmony with our God. We are confident that God will meet all our needs, regardless of what happens!

Do we want a life without fear? We can truly have that. All we need to do is delight in the fear of the Lord, and behold how our purity will be enhanced! Remember always Exodus 20:20 when Moses said, **"Do not be** *afraid. God has come to test you, so that the fear of God will be with you to keep you from sinning."*

Chapter 8
God Sees Us As Mighty Warriors

Happy are those whose way is blameless,
Who walk in the law of the Lord.
Happy are those who keep his decrees,
Who seek him with their whole heart.
(Psalm 119:1-2 NRSV)

While we may have momentary happiness with favorable circumstances like a good meal or a gift, even sexual sin, the problem is that it is only temporary. After we sin, we feel empty and wanting more just to satisfy our desires. In the long run, sexual sin makes us miserable and addicted. Oftentimes, we fall into impurity because we are not "happy" with our lives and desire some comfort. We erroneously believe that impurity and sexual sin will make us happy, when in fact they make us very unhappy and in the long run, can destroy our lives if we do not repent of them.

True happiness only comes from one source – a relationship with God. Only he can satisfy our deepest desires. Some have said, "We have a hole in our heart that only he can fill." True happiness is a by-product of seeking God. If we seek him with all our hearts, we will be given a deep joy that is not due to our circumstances. Even when we go through difficult ordeals, we can be at peace and "be happy" because it comes from our relationship with God.

Psalm 23:4 states,

> *Even though I walk through the*
> *darkest valley,*
> *I fear no evil;*
> *For you are with me;*
> *Your rod and your staff –*
> *They comfort me.*

One of the biggest challenges in our walk with God is to see ourselves the way our God sees us. Often, we have a "bad" view of ourselves as well as an erroneous view of God. This, in turn, leads us to be insecure in our walk with God, insecure with other people, and insecure with ourselves. It is ultimately the foothold that Satan uses for our downfall.

Satan is always attacking us so we see ourselves negatively. He wants us either to get insecure and depressed about ourselves, or get prideful and arrogant. Both extremes drive us away from God. We need to see ourselves exactly the same as God sees us. Satan even attacked Jesus in this manner while he was on earth.

> *When all the people were being*
> *baptized, Jesus was baptized too. And*
> *as he was praying, heaven was opened*
> *and the Holy Spirit descended on him*
> *in bodily form like a dove. And a voice*
> *came from heaven: "You are my Son,*
> *whom I love; with you I am well*
> *pleased." Now Jesus himself was about*
> *thirty years old when he began his*

ministry. (Luke 3:21-23)

Right after Jesus's baptism, the Father tells all watching in an audible voice, ***"You are my Son, whom I love; with you I am well pleased."*** God wanted everyone to know that Jesus was his one and only begotten son. He also wanted Jesus to hear these words and give him confidence to fulfil his earthly mission. Because Jesus was human (as well as God), he had all the human temptations that we all endure. One of them was doubting his calling and not seeing himself the way God saw him. God saw him as his son. This is precisely the area that Satan attacked him.

> ***The devil said to him, "If you are the Son of God, tell this stone to become bread." Jesus answered, "It is written: 'Man shall not live on bread alone.'" (Luke 4:3-4)***

This is an amazing temptation! ***"If you are the Son of God,"*** said Satan. Satan was implying that if Jesus was the Son of God he would turn the stones into bread. After all, Jesus must have been pretty hungry with his 40 day fast, and it was God's idea to bring Jesus into the desert to be tempted. Very interestingly, Satan wanted Jesus to doubt his identity because if he did, then Jesus would not have the faith to be the instrument of the salvation for the world or have the faith to die on the cross. If Satan could get Jesus to be insecure about who he was (the Son of God) and use his power prematurely to meet his own needs, then he could get Jesus to doubt God was good and would provide for his needs. In this case, the need was food.

This is exactly how Satan attacks Christians. He says to them, "You are God's son and you do not have a girlfriend or boyfriend. Is it really going to happen in the church? I don't think so. There is no one for you in the church to marry. Maybe God does not care for you as much as he says he does. You have to go out and get your own."

Sadly, many of us believe the lie and look for non-Christian men or women, falling into sexual sin with them. Or, we just go and watch pornography and masturbate because we think God cannot meet our desires. Some of us might reason: If he cannot meet our desires for a mate in our timing, that means God does not care for us that much. If we have had family members who did not care for us very much growing up, this realization has deep roots in our hearts. This opens the door for masturbation and pornography.

As a result, Satan gets a victory with us because he gets us to doubt our identity as Christians. Jesus did not give in to these temptations, because he could thus show us the way out. He did not doubt his identity; we need not doubt ours!

There are two additional temptations in this story. Let us look at them:

> **The devil led him to Jerusalem and had him stand on the highest point of the temple. "If you are the Son of God," he said, "throw yourself down from here. For it is written:**

He will command his angels concerning you
  To guard you carefully;
They will lift you up in their hands.
  So that you will not strike your foot against a stone."

Jesus answered, "It is said: 'Do not put the Lord your God to the test.'"

The devil led him up to a high place and showed him in an instant all the kingdoms of the world. And he said to him, "I will give you all their authority and splendor; it has been given to me, and I can give it to anyone I want to. If you worship me, it will all be yours." Jesus answered, "It is written: 'Worship the Lord your God and serve him only.'" (Luke 4:5-12)

Again, there are two similar temptations. *"If you are the Son of God, throw yourself down from the top of the temple because God will protect you,"* and *"If you are the Son of God, you deserve to rule all the kingdoms of the world. All you have to do is bow down to me."* These temptations are also grounded in an attack on Jesus's identity. Thank Jesus he overcame them because he was secure in who he was and who God is.

After these temptations, it says that:

Then the devil left him, and angels came and attended him. (Matthew 4:11)

If we persevere through temptations, God comforts us. Sometimes, he might even do that through angels as he did here with Jesus. After we are tempted and we persevere, God gives us a time of peace. But then comes the warning:

When the devil had finished all this tempting, he left him until an opportune time. (Luke 4:13)

Satan intended to return to Jesus to tempt him again. *This means that the temptation in doubting our identity before God and seeing ourselves the way God sees us is an ongoing life temptation.* The opportune time would be a time when Jesus would be weak, as when he had fasted 40 days and was hungry.

Satan wants us to see ourselves and God in an unhealthy way. If he can, it is just a matter of time until we think that our relationship with God does not fulfil us, and thus we look to things in the world to fill that gap in our lives. Sadly enough, sexual sin is where the majority of us go to get that fulfilment. The challenge in our lives is to see ourselves the way God sees us. Two vital questions then becomes: How does God see us? And how should we see God?

He is our father in the sight of God, in whom he believed – the God who gives life to the dead and calls into being

things that were not. (Romans 4:17)

God sees what is not there. He saw the multitudes of Abraham's descendants before they were there. God has vision for our lives. He does not see us as we are. We may see ourselves as full of sin, imperfect, not good enough, lacking and constantly failing. He does not see us like that. He sees how we are not, but in positive ways. He sees us as his awesome sons and daughters in whom he delights. He loves us deeply. He does not only love us, he also likes us as well. He loves contemplating how awesome we are. This is the way a Christian parent sees his children, even though as parents we can see our children's faults and shortcomings.

When the angel of the Lord appeared to Gideon, he said, "The Lord is with you, mighty warrior." (Judges 6:12)

God saw Gideon as a mighty warrior. The problem was that at this time, Gideon was not a warrior at all. In fact, instead of fighting, he was hiding from Israel's enemies who were the Midianites. God did not see him as he was, but as how he could be in the future.

Likewise, God sees all of us as mighty warriors for him! If God chooses to see us like this, how should we see ourselves? We need to see ourselves as the "delight of God" because we are Christians. Yes, we are not perfect, but we are his sons and daughters. Because of our imperfections, he sent Jesus to die for us. He did not send Jesus to die for us so we could be depressed and down all the time and think we are worthless. No! He sent Jesus so we could be *"more than conquerors"* (Romans 8:37) and make an eternal impact in this world as we eagerly await for him to receive us in heaven.

If God has vision for us, we need to have vision for ourselves. As it says in Proverbs 29:18 (KJV):

> *Where there is no vision, the people perish.*

We all agree we should have vision for the church and for our brothers and sisters. This is usually not so hard to do. What is hard, indeed, is to have "vision" for ourselves. It is imperative that we gain that vision because God already has it!

In Proverbs 23:7 (KJV), it reads:

> *For as he thinketh in his heart, so is he.*

Ultimately, this is the key to being a successful Christian. The way we think about ourselves is, in essence, what we will become. If we think we are insecure, we will become insecure. If we think we are not good enough, then we will not be good enough. On the other hand, if we think we are awesome because of God, then we will become awesome. If we think we are a precious son or daughter of God, then that will be our identity, and we will be secure Christians able to handle any and all challenges that are thrown our way, because God loves us and always has a way out. Also, we need to remember that any and all challenges are given or permitted by God for our ultimate good. They come so we can become more and more like Jesus and one day make it to heaven.

Again, how should we view God? In Isaiah 49:15-16 God says,

> *Can a mother forget the baby at her breast*
> *and have no compassion on the child she has borne?*
> *Though she may forget,*
> *I will not forget you!*
> *See, I have engraved you on the palms of my hands.*

Traditionally we believe that a mother's love for her child is the greatest love that exists. However, looking at this Scripture, we see otherwise. God loves us beyond any human mother or father ever could. God uses the metaphor of having Israel "engraved" on the palms of his hands. I like to think about God's omnipresence and omniscience at this point. For as much as parents love their children, they are not with them every single second of every day and they definitely do not know everything about the child. This human limitation does not apply to God. God knows and is very interested in every facet of our lives because he loves us. He also orchestrates all events for our ultimate good! (Romans 8:28) This points to God's omnipotence! God has all the power in the world to intervene in human affairs, and he does so all the time. The problem is that we do not realize it.

> *For God does speak – now one way, now*

another – though no one perceives it.
(Job 33:14)

God is always speaking to us, but as the Scripture says, we do not perceive it. We feel he is far, when in fact, he is quite close. The issue is that we do not see it as it really is! God speaks to us through his word, through other Christians, through life's circumstances, through blessings, and through challenges. He is always speaking to us. We just need to listen!

A conviction that totally changed and revolutionized the way I viewed God was understanding God's sovereignty. It took me about 14 years as a Christian to gain a conviction on God's sovereignty which consequently changed my view of God into a more positive one. What is the sovereignty of God mean? It means that God is in control of everything. God's sovereignty means that all the good things in our lives happened because he allows them. Even things we could say that we achieved with our own effort happened because of God. After all, he is the one who gave us the ability to put the "effort" in so we could accomplish something. It was indeed, God! When we realize that all good things come from God, then we are humble. This humility should give us an awe of God, which should lead us to draw closer to him. Good things come from God.

Don't be deceived, my dear brothers and sisters. Every good and perfect give is from above, coming down from the Father of the heavenly lights, who does not change like shifting shadows.

(James 1:16-17)

The Scripture says not to be deceived about this. Why? God knows that we do get deceived from time to time, and believe that the good things in our lives come from us and our efforts! This is not the case.

The second aspect of God's sovereignty that we need to grasp is a harder one, but essential nonetheless. It is extremely important for us to understand the sovereignty of God through trials. We need to understand that all the bad things that happen in our lives are either caused by God or allowed by God for our ultimate good!

This is quite difficult! Most of us, when we suffer, stray from God and even blame him for wrongdoing because of our sufferings. It reminds me of the Scripture in Revelation 16:8-11,

> *The fourth angel poured out his bowl on the sun, and the sun was allowed to scorch people with fire. They were seared by the intense heat and they cursed the name of God, who had control over these plagues, but they refused to repent and glorify him.*

> *The fifth angel poured out his bowl on the throne of the beast, and its kingdom was plunged into darkness. People gnawed their tongues in agony and cursed the God of heaven because of their pains and their sores, but they*

refused to repent of what they had done.

The fourth and fifth angel poured God's wrath on the earth, and people suffered. Unfortunately, all that suffering was in vain, because the people refused to repent. Instead of repenting, they became even more bitter towards God and in their pride had the audacity to curse God!

This is who we are in our pride. We do not like to be corrected. We do not like to be disciplined. We do not like to submit even if the one we are submitting to is God himself. We want to do things our way. This is such, because we have a wrong view about God's nature and intentions. We believe that correction is bad for the most part. Maybe this is because we have had people and family members correct us in anger, or we have had our lives exposed to those who had little or no regard for us and wanted to hurt us. This is true in this world from a human point of view, but with God, who is sovereign over this world, it is much different. God loves us, and his discipline is for our good. God does not want to discipline us because he does not like us. Quite the opposite, he disciplines us because he loves us!

Make every effort to live in peace with everyone and to be holy; without holiness no one will see the Lord. See to it that no one falls short of the grace of God and that no bitter root grows up to cause trouble and defile many. See that no one is sexually immoral, or is

godless like Esau. (Hebrews 12:14-16)

This incredible passage teaches that we can miss the grace of God as a Christian. This is pretty intense. How can we miss the grace of God? If we miss the grace of God, then we are no longer saved! We would sadly lose our salvation. We can miss the grace of God by allowing bitterness to take root in our hearts. When we are bitter it not only affects ourselves, but also others around us as well.

What is bitterness and why is it so bad? Bitterness is handling life's sufferings in an unhealthy way. We do not accept the suffering or trial that we are going through. Instead we say things like: "It is not fair. It is too much. Why me?" Since we do not accept it, we end up blaming people for our suffering. We may even blame ourselves and fall into depression. Ultimately, we blame God. Even if we do not say it, we are angry at God for the way our lives turned out. We do not believe that God is sovereign and is allowing or causing this suffering for our ultimate good.

When we do not believe that God is sovereign, we will be bitter. Someone once said, "Bitterness is drinking the poison and wanting another person to die." Bitterness eats you from the inside out and affects every facet of our lives and all of our relationships. This is because we do not trust God. We do not see God as good. We see him as unfair at best, evil at worst! Because of this, we desire comfort to make up for what we consider unfair. That comfort, unfortunately, usually comes from sexual sin. We give ourselves to sexual sin and thus reap intense consequences because of it.

What is the solution to this problem that all humans face? Sadly, the older we become, the more bitter most people are. The solution is to change our view of God! We can change our view of God by drawing closer to him and understanding his sovereignty. Let us consider Hebrews 12:3-7:

> **Consider him who endured such opposition from sinners so that you will not grow weary and lose heart. In your struggle against sin, you have not yet resisted to the point of shedding your blood. And have you completely forgotten this word of encouragement that addresses you as a father addresses his son? It says,**
>
> **"My son, do not make light of the Lord's discipline,**
> **and do not lose heart when he rebukes you,**
> **because the Lord disciplines the one he loves,**
> **and he chastens everyone he accepts as his son."**
>
> **Endure hardship as discipline; God is treating you as his children. For what children are not disciplined by their father?**

This passage of Scripture is pivotal to understanding

the sovereignty of God. First, it states that if we are *"weary"* and have *"lost heart,"* there is a reason for that. The reason is that we are not looking at Jesus! Jesus had to suffer more than we ever suffered or will ever suffer, yet he was without sin. Why? Because he kept his eyes on his Father! Growing weary and losing heart means that we are tired of life, sad and depressed. None of us as Christians have had to shed our blood for Jesus, although there might be a few exceptions. But none of us will ever suffer like Jesus did. We have nothing to complain about when we compare our lives to Jesus. Really, there is no comparison at all.

Then, the Scripture above goes further into explaining that we have forgotten the words of encouragement that are addressed to us as sons. God says that we forgot. We forget God's words of encouragement for us who are his sons and daughters. When we think about words of encouragement, what comes to mind? Surely, they are words that lift us up? These are surely words that invigorate us and boost our self-confidence, that cheer us up, console us, energize us, revitalize us, fortify us, and inspire us to do great things.

However, God's words of encouragement are very different from our definitions of encouragement! Remember the Scripture:

> *My son, do not make light of the Lord's discipline,*
> *And do not lose heart when he rebukes you,*
> *Because the Lord disciplines the one he loves,*

*And he chastens everyone he accepts
as his son.*

God's words of encouragement are his discipline. It says that his encouragement is disciplining those he accepts as his sons and daughters. God loves us so much that he will discipline us. Just as a father disciplines his children because it is good for them, so God will discipline us because he loves us, and he knows we need discipline in our lives so that we can become more like Jesus and ultimately make it to heaven.

Our Lord Jesus Christ was no exception to discipline in his life. Even though Jesus is God, when he was on earth, some of his learning was to be progressive in nature, because he decided to accept God's limits on himself when he became a human being. Jesus had to learn through suffering. Let us consider Hebrews 5:7-9:

> *During the days of Jesus's life on earth, he offered up prayers and petitions with fervent cries and tears to the one who could save him from death, and he was heard because of his reverent submission. Son though he was, he learned obedience from what he suffered and, once made perfect, he became the source of eternal salvation for all who obey him.*

Jesus learned obedience through the suffering he experienced! The same principle applies to us. "All hardship" or suffering in our lives is for the sake of us learning obedience, so we could become more like Jesus. That is why sufferings and hardships are supposed to be seen as an encouragement from God. God is using the hardships to get you to be more and more like Jesus. Do you delight in your weaknesses? Paul did! And you can, too!

That is why, for Christ's sake, I delight in weaknesses, in insults, in hardships, in persecutions, in difficulties. For when I am weak, then I am strong. (2 Corinthians 12:10)

We need to change our view of suffering. We will only do so when we change our view of God. God is sovereign in our sufferings. This means that everything that is bad in our lives is either caused by God or allowed by him for our good. All the bad things in our lives are for our good, even if they cause us pain now. This is true even if we cannot understand our suffering at this point in time. That is why when we suffer, we have to ask ourselves a fundamental question: What good is God trying to teach us through this hardship?

If we see God as sovereign in both blessing and hardships, then we will lead happy and productive Christian lives. Life, in fact, becomes an adventure. There is a sense of excitement in life, as we see God guiding us in every facet of our lives, and as we pray for wisdom to understand what God is trying to teach us. This is the way to overcome bitterness in our lives. If we can overcome bitterness by seeing ourselves the way God sees us, then we can overcome any and all sexual sin, since we will see God clearly, and that He is on our side and always looking out for us! Get ready to live an exciting and invigorating Christian life, as we see God sovereign over all the world and over everything in our lives!

Chapter 9
Hating Defeat

Someone once said this describes a fool's mindset: "How close can you get to the fire without being burned?" We all need to be humble in understanding the nature of sexual temptation. If we are putting ourselves in a position where we are getting tempted sexually on a daily basis, we will most likely fall in time. No one knew this better than Joseph. In Genesis 39:6-10,

> *Now Joseph was well-built and handsome, and after a while his master's wife took notice of Joseph and said, "Come to bed with me!" But he refused. With me in charge," he told her, "my master does not concern himself with anything in the house; everything he owns he has entrusted to my care. No one is greater in this house than I am. My master has withheld nothing from me except you, because you are his wife. How then could I do such a wicked thing and sin against God?" And though she spoke to Joseph day after day, he refused to go to bed with her or even be with her.*

This is an amazing account about a great man of purity! Potiphar's wife openly invited Joseph to have sex with her. But Joseph refused. He says, *"How then could I do such a wicked thing and sin against God?"* Joseph saw sinning against God as wicked and perverse. He hated the thought of sinning against God. He hated evil. He hated the fact that sin could defeat him. Therefore, he did not allow sin to defeat him!

How can we imitate Joseph's mindset about sinning against God in a sexual way? We have to hate evil and the defeat it causes. Sin is defeat! Until we hate sexual sin, we will not change. Why do we not change? We do not change because we love our sin more than God! This is very tough to say, but we have to come to grips with it. We simply have to hate sin! This is the theme throughout the Bible. Let us look at two passages:

> *Love must be sincere. Hate what is evil;*
> *cling to what is good. (Romans 12:9)*

How do we know if we have a sincere love for God? We have to hate what is evil! If we do not hate what is evil, our love for God is not complete. Impurity and sexual immorality are evil. We need to hate these practices! God does! He hates them because these sins hurt us. We also must hate sexual sin because it hurts all people who practice them.

> *To fear the Lord is to hate evil.*
> *(Proverbs 8:13)*

It is hard to say that we should hate as Christians, but we should. We should hate the things that God hates, and God hates sin. If we change our mindset, we will overcome sexual sin.

There are six things the Lord hates, seven that are detestable to him: haughty eyes, a lying tongue, hands that shed innocent blood, a heart that devises wicked schemes, feet that are quick to rush into evil, a false witness who pours out lies, and a person who stirs up conflict in the community. (Proverbs 6:16-19)

There are things, and I dare say even people, that God hates. God hates because of his immense love. He hates the things that damage the world that he has created. He hates the things that drive people away from him. It is an act of love! When we love someone, we want to protect that person.

Now, let us revisit the story of Joseph for a minute. Joseph had convictions about purity. He ran out of the house when he was tempted. Why? Because he probably knew that if he stayed in the house with Potiphar's wife, he had a good chance of falling into sin. He was probably attracted to her. Joseph was radical with sexual temptation. The fact that he was radical with sin did not exempt him from being attracted to the opposite sex. After all, temptation is not sin. But really, we have to ask ourselves a fundamental question: How radical are we?

Some Christians flirt, and then they wonder why they fell into sin. Flirting is sin. Potiphar's wife was going beyond flirting and into sexual harassment, but Joseph stood firm. What would we do if someone in our class or at work was constantly flirting with us or giving us sexual innuendos? What do we do when someone sends us inappropriate text messages? What do we do when we are put in an uncomfortable sensual situation by a friend, coworker, stranger or even a family member?

Not doing anything is not a solution! We have to be radical like Joseph. We need to tell the person to stop! If they do not listen, we need to tell someone in authority like a teacher, boss or parents if the case applies. We need to be radical! If we are in a situation in which there is no one in authority to help, we have to be like Joseph. We have to run out of there. We may have to lose a job or change a class. Again, it is worth being radical. Why? We do not want to fall into sin, and we also want to protect ourselves from the consequences of giving into the attacking party.

If we allow ourselves to be put into a situation in which we are tempted daily, eventually something bad will happen. We will be hurt in one way or another if we do not do anything. An example of this is Samson. He allowed himself to be put into a situation in which he was tempted daily in Judges 16:15-17, 20-22,

> *Then she said to him, "How can you say, 'I love you,' when you won't confide in me? This is the third time you have made a fool of me and haven't told me the secret of your great strength." With such nagging she prodded him day after day until he was sick to death of it. So he told her everything. "No razor has ever been used on my head,"*

he said, "because I have been a Nazirite dedicated to God from my mother's womb. If my head were shaved, my strength would leave me, and I would become as weak as any other man...

Then she called, "Samson, the Philistines are upon you!" He awoke from his sleep and thought, "I'll go out as before and shake myself free." But he did not know that the Lord had left him. Then the Philistines seized him, gouged out his eyes and took him down to Gaza. Binding him with bronze shackles, they set him to grinding grain in the prison. But the hair on his head began to grow again after it had been shaved.

This passage is very sad! Samson allowed himself to be tempted daily by Delilah. Her daily nagging almost drove him crazy, and he ultimately told her the secret of his great strength. He ended losing his eyes and became a prisoner of the Philistines and eventually lost his life! Samson should not have put himself in his position in the first place. Samson should have repented. He should have left Delilah who was not part of God's people. After all, true Christians should only date and marry true Christians. (1 Corinthians 7:39) But Samson thought he was strong emotionally, and he finally fell. Samson was arrogant. As it says in 1 Corinthians 10:12, *"So, if you think you are standing firm, be careful that you don't fall!"* Let us learn from both Joseph and from Samson what we should do and what we should not do, so we may remain pure for our Lord Jesus Christ!

Chapter 10
The Repentant Soldier

Everyone has a need to repent. Even soldiers! As Christians we are soldiers for Christ. Interestingly, repentance is a concept that is not understood by most. Even in religious circles, it is not understood. What is repentance? What does it mean to repent? Most people think that repentance means to feel bad for sinning or simply feeling remorse. That could not be further from the truth! The word repentance in Greek is *metanoia*. *Metanoia* literally means afterthought, from *meta* meaning after or beyond and *noia* meaning "mind." In Classical Greek, *metanoia* meant changing one's mind about someone or something. [1]

As we can see, repentance in the Greek means to change one's mind. That change of mind will undoubtedly lead us to change our life.

> *Do not conform to the pattern of this world, but be transformed by the renewing of your mind. Then you will be able to test and approve what God's will is – his good, pleasing and perfect will. (Romans 12:2)*

Changing our minds is what truly changes us because some people can change their actions for superficial reasons, but deep in their hearts they do not think differently. Once we change our thinking about something, it is much easier for our actions to follow.

Let us look at an example of someone who did not repent Judas!

When Judas, who had betrayed him, saw that Jesus was condemned, he was seized with remorse and returned the thirty pieces of silver to the chief priests and the elders. "I have sinned," he said, "for I have betrayed innocent blood."

"What is that to us?" they replied. "That's your responsibility."

So Judas threw the money into the temple and left. Then he went away and hanged himself. (Matthew 27:3-5)

The question becomes: Did Judas repent? Some say that he did. If the definition of repentance is feeling bad about sin, then he did indeed repent. But as we have just seen, repentance is changing our mind in a way that changes our actions. The bottom line is that Judas did not repent. He had remorse about his sin. That means that he felt bad about his sin. Feeling bad about our sin is not the same as repentance! This is why many people do not change in lasting, dynamic ways.

Many feel badly when they sin sexually, but they do not change. Just feeling bad about our sin is not good enough, although we do need to feel remorse when we sin. Judas also made some superficial changes when he decided first to return the 30 pieces of silver to the chief priests, and secondly, to confess to them that he had sinned betraying innocent blood that is the innocent blood of Jesus!

Like Judas, some when they sin sexually, make some changes. These changes do not endure, and thus they prevent the person from truly repenting. A good Scripture about Biblical repentance is 2 Corinthians 7:8-11,

> *Even if I caused you sorrow by my letter, I do not regret it. Though I did regret it – I see that my letter hurt you, but only for a little while – yet now I am happy, not because you were made sorry, but because your sorrow led you to repentance. For you became sorrowful as God intended and so were not harmed in any way by us. Godly sorrow brings repentance that leads to salvation and leaves no regret, but worldly sorrow brings death. See what this godly sorrow has produced in you: what earnestness, what eagerness to clear yourselves, what indignation, what alarm, what longing, what concern, what readiness to see justice done. At every point you have proved yourselves to be innocent in this matter.*

There is sorrow when we sin. This is necessary for repentance, unless our conscience is seared, and we no longer feel anything when we sin. Not feeling badly when we sin is a very dangerous place to be. However, generally speaking, we all feel "badly" when we sin. This is what sorrow is all about. It is feeling a sadness and a disappointment when we sin. Notwithstanding, there are two types of sorrows we may have when we sin. We may either have worldly sorrow or godly sorrow.

Worldly sorrow leads to death because we either "die" spiritually and fall away or die physically. Both these things sadly happened to Judas. Judas is the classic example of someone who feels worldly sorrow when they sin. When we have worldly sorrow, we feel down and that there is no hope. We really do not feel that we can change, so we might as well sin some more sexually, and enjoy our sin some more. In fact, that can become our only source of enjoyment if we turn away from God. People who have worldly sorrow enter into a downward spiral of sadness "acedia" and depression and do not change. Because they do not change, they keep falling into sexual sin because they fundamentally believe that it is too late for them. There is no hope. This is one of Satan's traps to get a Christian to fall away!

We are also plagued by a false sense of honesty and honor, and we can think something along these lines, "If I can't stop sinning, I might as well leave the church and not become a burden to the brothers and sisters." This is not how God wants us to feel. If any of us are feeling this way now and are tempted to leave, please do not! We need to understand that with God, there is always hope to change. The way to change is to have godly sorrow!

What is godly sorrow? To start with, we feel sad when we sin, but the great thing godly sorrow is that it leads us to repentance. It leads to repentance because of what it causes in us. It produces earnestness and eagerness to clear ourselves. We just want to be different. We want to see justice done in the sense of restitution to those that we have sinned against. Someone who displayed godly sorrow was Zacchaeus when he was called by Jesus to dine with him:

> **But Zacchaeus stood up and said to the Lord, "Look, Lord! Here and now I give half of my possessions to the poor, and if I have cheated anybody out of anything, I will pay back four times the amount."**

> **Jesus said to him, "Today salvation has come to this house, because this man, too, is a son of Abraham. For the Son of Man came to seek and to save what is lost." (Luke 19:8-10)**

This is repentance! Zacchaeus would give half of his possessions to the poor and pay back those he had cheated four times the amount. That is amazing! This indeed is a man changed in his thinking! This is how we know if we have repented. We have godly sorrow and it leads us to change our lives. We then take dramatic steps in that direction and make amends and restitution for our sins when possible.

Another aspect of repentance not often talked about is

the concept of indignation that is self-indignation. As said before, when we sin sexually or when we sin in any way for that matter, we have the tendency to get sad and down and depressed. We rarely repent or change in this emotional state. Self-indignation is anger at ourselves. This anger does not lead us to hate ourselves, but rather the opposite. This "anger" leads us to hate our sin and change radically. I guess I can explain this in terms of a soldier in battle. If we are in a war, and we are a little bit injured, what do we do? Do we just get sad and down, and just allow the enemy to capture us or kill us? No! We need to get upset and fight back. We need to get that internal anger that comes from a healthy view of ourselves and fight back. This is what this kind of Biblical indignation is all about when we sin. It leads us to make radical changes and truly repent. It leads us to be a penitent soldier! This is how we need to feel when we sin. Let us imitate the heart of Zacchaeus when we sin, and let us enjoy the fruit that comes from godly sorrow in our lives, so we can give glory to God!

Chapter 11
The Soldier Who Forgave Himself

We all sin, unfortunately! However, besides the fact that God forgives us, we need to learn something very important. We need to learn to forgive ourselves. Every good soldier for Christ needs to learn to forgive himself or herself.

Guilt is a very powerful emotion. It is an emotion that must be handled correctly if we are to overcome sexual sin. There is a difference between guilt and guilty feelings. When we sin, we are guilty because it is our responsibility. Guilty feelings are another thing entirely. Sometimes we use the word shame to describe these guilty feelings. These are the feelings we get when we do something wrong. Those feelings can be exaggerated or they can be minimized, but nonetheless, we all get these feelings when we sin.

Satan attacks us through our guilty feelings when we sin sexually because many of us have an accused personality. An accused personality is the person who already feels guilty even before he sins. He may even be deceived and think that temptations are sin and feel bad, even though he has not sinned.

Now have come the salvation and the power and the kingdom of our God, and the authority of his Messiah. For the accuser of our brothers and sisters, who accuses them before our God day

and night, has been hurled down.
(Revelation 12:10)

The Bible teaches that Satan accuses Christians before God both day and night. His name literally means "accuser." His plan is for us to live with an accused conscience as well. At this, he is very good. Many Christians live with overdeveloped guilty consciences and feel badly about their sins all the time. They feel very accused and do not understand the grace of God and the freedom that comes with it.

> *Then he showed me Joshua the high priest standing before the angel of the Lord, and Satan standing at his right side to accuse him... Now Joshua was dressed in filthy clothes as he stood before the angel. The angel said to those who were standing before him. "Take off his filthy clothes."*
>
> *Then he said to Joshua, "See, I have taken away your sin, and I will put fine garments on you."*
>
> *Then I said, "Put a clean turban on his head." So they put a clean turban on his head and clothed him, while the angel of the Lord stood by. (Zechariah 3:1, 3-5)*

In this great vision, we see Joshua the high priest dressed in *"filthy clothes."* The *"filthy clothes"* were representative of his sins. The angel of the Lord, however, took off the *"filthy clothes"* and put fine garments on him. He took away his sin and his guilt. He was no longer to be in an accused state.

This is exactly what Jesus does to us when we are born again. He takes away our sin and our guilt, so we do not have to live with an accused conscience. This is very good. But the sad thing is that many of us persist in our guilty conscience even though God has already forgiven us.

An accused conscience can lead to more sin. Let us look at another example in the Scriptures. Let us look at Isaiah.

> *"Woe to me!" I cried. "I am ruined! For I am a man of unclean lips, and I live among a people of unclean lips, and my eyes have seen the King, the Lord Almighty."*
>
> *Then one of the seraphim flew to me with a live coal in his hand, which he had taken with tongs from the altar. With it he touched my mouth and said, "See, this has touched your lips, your guilt is taken away and your sin atoned for." (Isaiah 6:5-7)*

Here, we have the same incredible insight about guilt that is very similar to the former passage! When God forgives, he takes away our sin and our guilt, as in the case of Isaiah amidst this awesome vision! We are no longer guilty nor should our guilty feelings remain.

What we should have at this point is gratitude. When Jesus forgives us, we no longer need to remain guilty and beat ourselves. Romans 8:1 states, *"Therefore, there is now no condemnation for those who are in Christ Jesus."* There is no condemnation because Jesus took all of our sins on the cross and bore all the guilt. When we sin as disciples, we need to understand this Scripture:

> *This is the message we have heard from him and declare to you: God is light, in him there is no darkness at all. If we claim to have fellowship with him and yet walk in the darkness, we lie and do not live out the truth. But if we walk in the light, as he is in the light, we have fellowship with one another, and the blood of Jesus, his Son, purifies us from all sin.*
>
> *If we claim to be without sin, we deceive ourselves and the truth is not in us. If we confess our sins, he is faithful and just and will forgive us our sins and purify us from all unrighteousness. If we claim we have not sinned, we make him out to be a liar and his word is not in us. (1 John 1:5-10)*

This is an amazing Scripture! There is a huge difference in sinning as a Christian as opposed to sinning as a non-Christian. Once we are saved and have a saved relationship with God being as his sons and daughters, the blood of Christ continues to purify us from all sin.

This means that our sins committed after we are saved are forgiven. This is amazing! All we need to do is to walk in the light. Walking in the light means being a disciple of Jesus and not giving up. Part of doing that is confessing our sins to God and to our brothers and not hiding sin in our hearts.

This means that when we sin as a Christian, we are forgiven! But this sounds too good to be true. From a certain point of view, it is too good to be true, but it is nonetheless true. There is a part of us that does not want to accept this grace. We want to feel guilty. We want to beat ourselves. We want to feel down. We want to inflict self-harm for the sin we have committed. This is why the guilty soul keeps falling into sin. He does not accept the grace of God when he sins sexually, and he feels that he has failed God.

If we just understood Jesus's grace for us after salvation, it would protect our hearts from a guilty conscience, and we would definitely sin a lot less in the sexual area, because we would be motivated by his love. After all, we do not want to hurt those whom we love deeply, and no one loves us more than God!

Moreover, when God forgives us our sin, he decides to forget even though he is omniscient. God's omniscience means that he knows everything. But just like a loving father, God decides to forgive us and forget our sins when we sin as Christians. In Hebrews 8:12,

For I will forgive their wickedness

And will remember their sins no more.

This is absolutely amazing! The problem is that we do not forgive ourselves, but we need to! Our guilty souls and accused personalities will lead us to beat ourselves and to keep feeling down and depressed when we sin, or even when we are not sinning. Forgiving ourselves is essential to becoming pure.

One of the reasons we do not forgive ourselves has to do with the frequency of our sin. We may say, "I just masturbated last week, and now I did it again and watched pornography. Am I even a Christian? I might as well leave the church because I am damaged goods. I have not changed and will never change. I cannot change. I am already condemned." I know this type of thinking is pretty dark. However, many of us "go there" when we are not doing well spiritually. The guilt kills us, and it becomes Satan's tool to damage us spiritually, and sadly in many cases, even leave God! This all stems from not having a correct understanding of God's nature and how he sees us, and how we should see ourselves!

The other negative extreme is to feel no guilt when we sin. People who are like that are spiritual sociopaths.

Now, some may say, "If we are forgiven as Christians after we sin, then, can we do whatever we want?" We know deep inside that this question does not make sense. How can we abuse the grace of God and think everything is ok? There are many Scriptures that talk against sinning deliberately.

There is a point when we persist in sinning, that we eventually fall away! The guilty soul, however, gets to this point rather quickly and prematurely, and a lot quicker than God does. The guilty soul thinks he already fell away when he sins and especially when he sins sexually. Let us look at a Scripture in James:

> *When tempted, no one should say, "God is tempting me." For God cannot be tempted by evil, nor does he tempt anyone; but each person is tempted when they are dragged away by their own evil desire and enticed. Then, after desire has conceived, it gives birth to sin; and sin, when it is full-grown, gives birth to death. (James 1:13-15)*

First of all, God does not tempt anyone. Here, we see three stages of sins. These insights will change your life: The first stage is evil desires. The second stage is the sin itself. This is sin like masturbation, pornography or perhaps flirting at work, or sadly for some, sexual immorality! The third stage is full-grown sin that leads to death. This *"death"* is a spiritual one. This *"death"* means falling away, although we can die physically as a consequence of our sins as well! Now, falling away from God does not happen quickly. It is a process.

If we understand the Scripture above correctly, that would mean that if we sin, we have not fallen away from God! If we sin, we are still saved, even before confessing our sin and repenting. It is only when we reach the stage of full-grown sin that we fall away, and it goes without saying that we have to confess our sin and repent of it, so that we do not get to that third stage of sin and do indeed fall away. However, when we sin, we are not doing badly with God. Some think something along these lines, "I just masturbated and I am separated from God. When I confess and repent, I am "in the 'light' again and I am saved." This is not true. We do not go from "saved" to "unsaved" when we sin. And then when we confess and repent, we go from "unsaved" to "saved" once again. That would mean that we are saved by our actions or our works, which is impossible.

This doctrinal confusion stems from not understanding Isaiah 59:1-2,

> **Surely the arm of the Lord is not too short to save,**
> **Nor his ear too dull to hear.**
> **But your iniquities have separated you from your God;**
> **Your sins have hidden his face from you,**
> **So that he will not hear.**

The context of this Scripture is God talking to the Israelite nation that had fallen away from God because their sins. This does not mean that every time we sin, we fall away from God. We are still sons and daughters of God when we sin. Yes, we need to repent when we sin because we love God and do not want to hurt him. Also, we need to fear sinning because God will discipline us as a loving father, but he disciplines us

121

precisely because we are still his children when we sin, and because he loves us. Now we know that unsaved people are separated from God because their sins are not forgiven, but that is not the case with the Christian.

Oddly enough, if we were to die in the midst of sin, we would be saved if: 1) We are not living in sin, and 2) We have not reached the point of full-grown sin, which is falling away. For example, if a true Christian and gives into masturbation, and he gets a heart attack and dies in the midst of his masturbation, he would go to heaven because he is not living in sin. I know that sounds hard to believe, but it is true. This understanding of God's love for us and his grace motivates us to sin much less – not more! Our status as sons of God does not fluctuate every time we sin. If we are Christians, we are his sons; this sonship is a privilege.

But when we do cross that fine line of sinning to the point of falling away? Christians with a guilty conscience tend to think they have crossed that line prematurely when they have not. But when do we cross that line? After all, are we not in a fallen state as humans? Yes! We are! There is a concept that can help us understand this. The concept is: Sinning versus living in sin!

The letter of 1 John explains this dichotomy:

> *This is the message we have heard from him and declare to you: God is light; in him there is no darkness at all. If we claim to have fellowship with him and yet walk in the darkness, we lie*

and do not live out the truth. (1 John 1:5-6)

The Scriptures here talk about "walking in darkness versus walking in the light." If we walk in the darkness, we are not Christians according to this Scripture. Why is that? Anyone who is walking in the darkness is living in sin. They really do not care anymore about not sinning against God. Their sin does not hurt them. They are just putting on a show and acting as Christians when they are around the brothers and sisters, but secretly, they are living in sin. Their motivation to be at church is not to please God, but rather the benefit they get from relationships. Maybe they have their wife in the church. Or maybe they are lonely, and like the affection they receive from the friendships in the church. Or maybe they are teens, and they are in the church because they want to please their parents, but they really do not want to be there. People in these and other similar categories, live a life of sin hidden from the church. Usually, it is sexual sin but is not limited to it. They may be having sex or habitually masturbating and/or constantly watching pornography. Their sin is rampant, and they do not want to get caught. They are living a double life in the church. According to the Scripture above, they are living in darkness. This person is not saved even though he may be in the church and "act" as a disciple of Jesus and have positive characteristics. This is true because what they care about most are their relationships in the church and not their relationship with God. The way for them not to lose their relationships in the church is to pretend to be a Christian, but then they must hide their sin.

The identifying characteristic of someone living in darkness is not the fact that they hide their sin, but rather the fact that they do not feel badly about it. They have no shame when they sin. Jeremiah 6:15 says:

> *Are they ashamed of their detestable conduct?*
> *No, they have no shame at all;*
> *They do not even know how to blush.*
> *So they will fall among the fallen;*
> *They will be brought down when I punish them,"*
> *Says the Lord.*

This is the person who is living in unrepentant sin. Eventually, in most cases, their sins come out. They cannot hide it for too long, because their sexual sin has consequences. As I said before, the person living in sin is not saved.

Consider, also, these Scriptures in 1 John about living in sin. These words are very strong:

> *We know that we have come to know him if we keep his commands. Whoever says, "I know him," but does not do what he commands is a liar, and the truth is not in that person. But if anyone obeys his word, love for God is truly made complete in them. This is how we know we are in him: Whoever claims to live in him must live as Jesus did. (1 John 2:3-6)*

No one who is born of God will continue to sin, because God's seed remains in them; they cannot go on sinning, because they have been born of God. This is how we know who the children of God are and who the children of the devil are: Anyone who does not do what is right is not God's child, nor is anyone who does not love their brother and sister. (1 John 3:9-10)

The second category of people who live in the church are those who just "sin" but are still saved and forgiven. They do not live in sin, although they may fall into it and at times hide their sins out of shame. Yet these people need to beware, because they can also fall into sexual sins like pornography or masturbation or even sexual immorality, sadly. Let us look at 1 John 1:7 and 2:2,

But if we walk in the light, as he is in the light, we have fellowship with one another, and the blood of Jesus, his Son, purifies us from all sin.

If we claim to be without sin, we deceive ourselves and the truth is not in us. If we confess our sins, he is faithful and just and will forgive us our sins and purify us from all unrighteousness. If we claim we have not sinned, we make him out to be a liar and his word is not in us. My dear children, I write this to you so that you will not sin. But if anybody does sin, we

have an advocate with the Father –
Jesus Christ, the Righteous one. He is
the atoning sacrifice for our sins, and
not only for ours but also for the sins of
the whole world.

These are very comforting Scriptures. They basically teach that all Christians have sin. In fact, if we claim to have no sin, we are deceived, and God's truth is not in us. So, from this point of view, all Christians are continually sinning. Why? It is because we are in a fallen state, yet saved because of the blood of Jesus. This is true, because we are Christians. Let us remember that 1 John was written exclusively to Christians. It also teaches that if we do sin, it should not be constant practice. We have an advocate before the Father. This is Jesus! It is the very reason that Jesus died on the cross for us. We need constant forgiveness as disciples, and that is precisely the reason that Jesus died for us. Why is this so comforting to Christians? This is comforting because we all sin. And so, this brings us to the title of this chapter: "**The Soldier Who Forgives Himself.**" As disciples we can sin and still be right with God because we are not living in sin.

So, how do we know whether we are living in sin or just sinning? We know this by the heart and by the actions of the person that does indeed sin. If we are hiding sexual sin and we do not really feel bad about it, we are in trouble, especially if we only feel badly about getting caught. Usually, the person hiding sin in this way is caught in Satan's trap of sexual immorality, although it could also be masturbation, pornography, phone sex, etc. This is a sign that you are living in sin, and thus we are a fall away in the church.

Now, if we sin sexually like falling into masturbation and pornography, but we have godly sorrow and confess it, then the blood of Christ purifies us from all sin. This person that sins does not live in sin and is not falling into this sin every day. It is sporadic. He may fall into it once a month or once every two weeks or so. Obviously, the sin is ugly, but then again, all sin is. The Christian sinning but not living in sin is confessing and being open about this sin. He may be discouraged or even have a guilty conscience as we say in other chapters, but he is not living in sin. He is still saved, even though he may not feel that way because of his accused personality. He may have even from time to time have hidden sin, which is wrong, out of shame, but then he repents and decides to confess and be open with God and the brothers. The brother may even fall, sadly, into sexually immorality, but then he decides to repent and not do it again. He gets open with the brothers. He prays and he repents. He seeks God, and God grants his repentance.

This is an example of someone who just sins but is not living in sin! Without a doubt, this is a weak brother, but nonetheless a brother. There is a Scripture that shows us the difference between sinning and living in sin.

> *If you see any brother or sister commit a sin that does not lead to death, you should pray and God will give them life. I refer to those whose sin does not lead to death. There is a sin that leads to*

127

death. I am not saying that you should
pray about that. All wrongdoing is in,
and there is sin that does not lead to
death. (1 John 5:16-17)

Which is the sin that does not lead to death? It is the sin
from which we repent! The sin that leads to death is
the sin from which we do not repent. If we do not
repent from any sin, in particular sexual sin, it will lead
us to death and we will fall away. What is the difference
of sinning versus living in sin? Those who sin and do
not repent even when they get caught, they are the
ones that are living in sin and are thus, not being
purified by the blood of Jesus and are no longer
Christians.

On the other hand, those who sin sexually and repent
but then fall into the sin and repent again, those are the
ones who just sin and are not living in sin. They are still
saved, although they are weak Christians. Because they
are in the spiritual battle and they care, they are still
saved, and the blood of Christ continues to purify them
from all sin. Understanding this grace should lead us to
repent from sexual sin, because we see God's grace to
us in the midst of our sins. After all:

> *For the grace of God has appeared*
> *that offers salvation to all people. It*
> *teaches us to say "No" to ungodliness*
> *and worldly passions, and to live self-*
> *controlled, upright and godly lives in*
> *this present age. (Titus :10-12)*

Another thing that we need as soldiers with the

ultimate weapon of self-forgiveness is wisdom. We desperately need wisdom from above even when we sin. Let us consider the following passage:

> *Consider it pure joy, my brothers and sisters, whenever you face trials of many kinds, because you know that the testing of your faith produces perseverance. Let perseverance finish its work so that you may be mature and complete, not lacking anything. If any of you lacks wisdom, you should ask God, who gives generously to all without finding fault, and it will be given to you. But when you ask, you must believe and not doubt, because the one who doubts is like a wave of the sea, blown and tossed by the wind. That person should not expect to receive anything from the Lord. Such a person is double-minded and unstable in all they do. (James 1:2-8)*

This passage defines an unstable Christian. Basically, if we lack faith when we pray for help, we are unstable. The Bible here teaches that when we endure trials of any kind, we should be joyful. Trials of any kind would include the trials that we receive as a consequence of our sexual sin after we sin. The consequences of our sexual sin is a trial allowed by God to help us. Our faith is being tested so that, ultimately, we can be mature and not lack anything. Sexual sin is a lack of maturity. Maturity will help us overcome sexual sin. When we fall into sexual sin, we usually get down and enter a downward spiral of sadness and depression and self-pity. But the Scripture says to consider it pure joy when we go through trials. We need faith in the Scriptures to repent of sexual sin.

What is the faith that we need to have when we sin? We need to ask God for wisdom. To have wisdom is to have the ability to make good choices – discernment. We need to know how to act when we have sinned. We need to ask God and not doubt that he will answer our prayer in giving us wisdom so that we can overcome our sexual sin. If we pray to God and do not believe he will help us, we are unstable and our prayers will not be answered, and we will persist in our sin.

An example of getting this kind of wisdom from the Bible when we sin sexually, can be seen in 2 Corinthians 7:9-11,

> *Yet now I am happy, not because you were made sorry, but because your sorrow led you to repentance. For you became sorrowful as God intended and so were not harmed in any way by us. Godly sorrow brings repentance that leads to salvation and leaves no regret, but worldly sorrow brings death. See what this godly sorrow has produced in you: what earnestness, what eagerness to clear yourselves, what indignation, what alarm, what longing, what concern, what readiness to see justice done. At every point you have proved yourselves to be innocent*

in this matter.

When we sin, we will have sorrow or sadness. Worldly sorrow brings death. That means that we get so down when we sin, we feel like quitting. Some fall away from God because they believe they are hypocrites when they have sinned and do not feel worthy to be in the church. So they leave the church because of a twisted sense of honesty. Satan traps them in this way. That is one of the ways that worldly sorrow brings death.

But that is not the type of sorrow that God intended us to have when we sin. He intended us to have godly sorrow. Godly sorrow brings repentance. It produces an alarm and a longing to do what is right. It is the opposite of depression. It is the opposite of being ashamed because we look so bad in front of other men and women. Godly sorrow will make us determined to obey God and to change.

In conclusion, we need to not let our guilty conscience get us to quit on God because we are sinning sexually, and we feel that we have already fallen away. The fact that we are fighting shows that we are Christians and that we are still saved. Do not quit on God because he definitely does not want to quit on us!

Part Three
The Battle Of The Mind

Chapter 12
The Landmine Of Lust

For many years, I tried helping brothers to avoid pornography, masturbation and sexual immorality. But now, I realize that I was focusing on dealing with the "symptoms" rather than the "root" of the problem – something so vital in discipling. I was not focusing on the obvious underlying sin of lust. Lust is what leads to all the other sexual sins. Thus, falling into the sin of lust is like stepping onto a spiritual landmine that could lead us to explode, or dare we say implode, into all kinds of other sexual sins. We must radically crucify the sin of lust! Jesus said about lust:

> *But I tell you that anyone who looks at a woman lustfully has already committed adultery with her in his heart. If your right eye causes you to sin, gouge it out and throw it away. It is better for you to lose one part of your body than for your whole body to be thrown into hell. And if your right hand causes you to sin, cut it off and throw it away. It is better for you to lose one part of your body than for your whole body to go to hell. (Matthew 5:27-30)*

Jesus's goal was absolute purity. This must be our goal as well. The way to avoid the sins of pornography, masturbation and immorality is to deal decisively with the sin of lust. Lust by itself will take us to hell if we remain unrepentant. The intent of this passage is that we have to be radical and do whatever it takes to *"cut"* lust out of our lives. How radical are we about eliminating lust from our lives?

Have you ever had the following thoughts:

1) I will never overcome masturbation and pornography.
2) I will never be able to change these sins because I have not been able to overcome them for longer than two weeks.

There is good news if we feel like we will never overcome masturbation or pornography; give in to these sins regularly and feel like we will never be able to change; feel hopeless and defeated; consider falling away; "feel" like we will never change and that we can only hide this sin for so long before we get discovered; said we would change by ourselves time and time again and by our own effort, with nothing changing, with hidden sexual sin increasing in magnitude along with the lies that accompany it. There is hope! The hope is to battle the sin of lust with *"all our heart and with all our soul and with all our mind and with all our strength." (Mark 12:30)*

One of the ways to battle lust is to see the harm and hurt that it does to the people close to us. How would

133

our spouse, kids or girlfriend or boyfriend feel if they could see what goes through our minds as we look at women or men? Most importantly, how does God feel when we give in to lust? The hurt that it causes Him is huge! So huge that Jesus had to die on the cross and be separated from God because of it. The pain that we cause God and others with our lust and the sin that develops after that should lead us to repent. After all, we do not want to hurt those who we love. Ultimately, we have to choose which we love the most – our sin or our God.

Here are six practical things to do to overcome lust:

1. We need to make a purity covenant with God. *"I made a covenant with my eyes not to look lustfully at a girl."* (Job 31:1) This decision is first made at baptism when we declare, *"Jesus is Lord."* However, since we gave into impurity so often as non-Christians, for most the battle for purity is something entirely new. Therefore, I encourage every brother and sister to make a heartfelt vow to God to be totally pure. *"To do otherwise is to trample the Son of God under foot (and to treat) as an unholy thing the blood of the covenant that sanctified him."* (Hebrews 10:29)

2. We need to understand that attraction is not sin. *"God has made everything beautiful in its time."* (Ecclesiastes 3:11) The fact that we are attracted to the opposite sex is not sin. It is normal. Some have such a guilty conscience

that they already feel they have sinned if they see a beautiful women passing by. After this, they give in to sin believing that it is hopeless to change. My challenge is this: When we feel attracted to the opposite sex, acknowledge it. Then, take warning and move on. I see it as a "yellow alert." Set ourselves free from an overly guilty conscience.

3. <u>We need to hide God's Word in our hearts</u>. *"I have hidden your Word in my heart that I might not sin against you."* (Psalm 119:11) Meditating on God's word will keep us from lusting. How? Write Scriptures about purity on small index cards. When we are tempted, take them out and read them and combat the temptation with the most powerful weapon in the world: The Word of God. Better yet, memorize these Scriptures so that we can store them in our hearts and then call ourselves to obey them. (Proverbs 2:1)

4. <u>We need to pray Nehemiah Prayers</u>: *"Remember me with favor, O my God."* (Nehemiah 13:30) I love how Nehemiah prays to his God, especially when he first addressed the king about rebuilding the wall in Jerusalem. Immediately after, the king asked Nehemiah what he wanted. Nehemiah prayed as he made this incredible request. (Nehemiah 2:4) God favorably answered that prayer with the king's willingness to send him to Jerusalem. When tempted to lust, we need to pray in our minds

and in our hearts right then and there. God will give us the strength to overcome. (John 15:7)

5. <u>We need to cut off temptation.</u> *"Throw off everything that hinders and the sin that so easily entangles."* (Hebrews 12:1) If lust is our battle, we should *"throw off everything that (could) hinder"* our purity. For example, we need to strive never to use the internet when we are alone. We need to have a brother or sister or our spouse with us. Filters on the internet help, but we must still have the fear of God to keep us from sinning. (Exodus 20:20) Also, I recommend getting rid of the internet on our phones, because we are alone when we use it. We may have to get an old phone that does not have internet until we have radical victories over lust. It is unwise to watch television by ourselves, especially late at night. For some, they must be willing to get rid of their television or computer altogether if they are unable to be pure. This may sound radical, and it is! Is lust worth going to hell? Another sin that leads to lust is laziness. Our time outside of studies and work should be spent in the battle to win souls and in quality and fun fellowship activities. Laziness will kill us. Other practical things to not get entangled in lust are to only look at women or men in their eyes and share our faith with any woman or man that we feel attracted to at work or school. This helps maintain purity. And with sisters or brothers we may feel attracted to, be kind to them, but do not have long talks or we

will lust. Also, let the sisters disciple the sisters. They are more than capable of meeting their own needs. (Titus 2:2-4) As someone once said "The path to hell is paved with good intentions."

6. When a lustful thought enters our minds. *"You have heard it said, 'You shall not commit adultery.' But I tell you that anyone who looks at a woman lustfully has already committed adultery with her in his heart. If your right eye causes you to stumble, gouge it out and throw it away. It is better for you to lose one part of your body than for your whole body to be thrown into hell. And if your right hand causes you to stumble, cut it off and throw it away. It is better for you to lose one part of your body than for your whole body to go into hell."* (Matthew 5:27-30)

Lust can take us to hell! If we look lustfully at a woman or man, we have committed adultery with her or him in our hearts. If we persist in lusting, we will most definitely sin in other sexual ways. Now, looking at a woman or man lustfully is a conscious act. It is something that we decide to do. But how about when we just get a random lustful thought in our heads? Have we sinned? It is not simple.

Let us look at 2 Corinthians 10:5, *"We demolish arguments and every pretension that sets itself up against the knowledge of God, and we take captive every thought to make it obedient to Christ."*

This is an awesome Scripture because it says that we *"take every thought captive"* so the thought can ultimately be subject to Christ! To take captive a thought means that it is already in our minds. The thought is obviously there in our mind before we can capture it. That means that it is not sin if we just get a lustful thought all of the sudden. If we get an evil thought or a lustful thought, we have not sinned. However, we have to get that thought under control rather quickly before we are dragged away to sin. We have to capture it quickly by prayer and the truth of God's Word.

I recommend that we immediately pray in our minds for God to take the thought away. If we can pray audibly, it is much better. If not, so be it. Pray in our minds. Prayer is of the utmost need as a thought enters our minds. Then, reinforce our minds by reading Scriptures. Take our Bible out and read. Or just simply recite Scriptures from memory to combat this thought. An evil thought or an impure thought that just enters our mind is not sin. It is an attack by Satan! I came to this conclusion by thinking about other evil thoughts that can enter our minds and by meditating on the Scripture above. For example, if we have a suicidal thought, have we sinned just by having that thought? Think about it, if we get super guilty about having a suicidal thought, we may just commit suicide because we think there is no hope! But rather, if we perceive suicidal thoughts as evil thoughts that have entered our minds and as an attack by Satan, then we can take the proper steps to protect ourselves by prayer and Bible study.

One of the ways that Satan can bring us down is by playing on our exaggerated sense of guilt. I see this is the case with most people who struggle with lust. They already feel defeated when they have an impure, sinful thought, and so they decide to fall into masturbation, pornography and even sex. The solution is to fight the evil thoughts right away by capturing them. We need to fight evil thoughts with positive thoughts, and there is nothing more positive than the words of the Bible. As it says in Philippians 4:8, *"Finally, brothers and sisters, whatever is true, whatever is noble, whatever is right, whatever is pure, whatever is lovely, whatever is admirable – if anything is excellent or praiseworthy – think about such things."* We can also fight evil thought by singing a song that helps you think about God's word: Singing engages both the right and left sides of the brain, so we can literally love God with all our minds. Fill up the house with praise and those demons will not be able to come back worse than before!

7. We need to confess our sexual temptation and lust daily. *"Confess your sins to each other and pray for each other."* (James 5:17) This is God's safety mechanism against lust. Every night we need to confess to another brother or sister how

the day went in regards to lust and temptation. We should not by any means conceal lust even if we think it is small or inconsequential. We need to be radical and let the light shine into our darkness. A "little lust" in our minds will grow into other sins if we do not deal with it immediately. Proverbs 28:13 teaches, *"He who conceals his sins does not prosper, but whoever confesses and renounces them finds mercy."*

In conclusion, there is great hope for the disciple of Jesus who is radical with the sin of lust and avoids this spiritual landmine of Satan. As I look at my own life, I see many victories that my Father in heaven has given me because I have applied these seven principles. In my 20 years as a Christian, even though I have sinned with lust, neither pornography nor masturbation have been issues. Why? Was it because I was pure as a non-Christian? No! I was very impure and enslaved to the sins of pornography and masturbation, plus immorality! I believe strength comes in understanding how weak I am, and that only with Jesus can there be victory. One of the most powerful Scriptures for me about purity is: *"So, if you think you are standing firm, be careful that you do not fall."* (1 Corinthians 10:12) Strength comes from weakness. (2 Corinthians 12:9) I am so weak that I can fall tonight even after writing this, but with God's grace and power, nothing can stop me from pleasing God.

Chapter 13
Minds Prepared For Battle

I have spoken with many brothers who often fall into pornography and masturbation, and a good number of them have one thing in common, that there are periods during the day that they decide to think about nothing. They simply decide to leave their minds blank to relax from the day's pressures. Their minds are not prepared for the spiritual battle that rages around them every day. Their minds are idle! Not surprisingly, since their minds are blank or empty, Satan attacks them with lustful thoughts, and so they end up sinning by watching pornography and by masturbation.

The minds should never be empty. Matthew 12:43-45 states:

> *When an impure spirit comes out of a person, it goes through and places seeking rest and does not find it. Then it says, "I will return to the house I left." When it arrives, it finds the house unoccupied, swept clean and put in order. Then it goes and takes with it seven other spirits more wicked than itself, and they go in and live there. And the final condition of that person is worse than the first.*

Unfortunately, it seems that Satan has a contingency plan when he suffers defeat. The *"house"* in the

Scripture above represents us as people. When the impure spirit leaves, it desires to go back to his old **"house."** That is why he gets reinforcements recruiting other seven more powerful impure spirits to get back to his old house. Oddly enough, the **"house"** is unoccupied. The **"house"** is empty. This is not good. The Christian ends up worse than when the original impure spirit was in him because he was unoccupied. This could be interpreted as a Christian who gets converted, but then afterward gives in to laziness and selfishness and is not doing the work of God. Since this is the case, he is easy prey to Satan and ends up worse than before he was converted.

This applies to lust! If our minds are empty rooms and unoccupied, then Satan will occupy them with lustful thoughts. If we do not stop lust immediately, we will reach the point of "no return." At that point, we will give into masturbation and watching pornography or worse. That is why, as Christians, our minds cannot be empty. They always need to be occupied. We can never leave our minds empty to "relax," as that is a trap of Satan. Our relaxation comes from our relationship with God! Only God can give us rest.

What should we occupy our minds with?

> *Finally, brothers and sisters, whatever is true, whatever is noble, whatever is right, whatever is pure, whatever is lovely, whatever is admirable – if anything is excellent or praiseworthy – think about such things. (Philippians 4:8)*

142

This is what we should be thinking about: Things that are true, noble, right, pure, lovely, admirable, excellent, and praiseworthy. Some people accuse Christians of being brain-washed. About that charge, I say, absolutely yes! Our minds needed to be washed by God's Word and the good things about his kingdom.

Having said that, this verse shows us what we should think about. We need to keep our minds busy thinking about things that are godly. We need to keep our minds busy thinking about the things of God so we will be pure. Another Scripture is to consider this:

> **Be, filled with the Spirit, speaking to one another with psalms, hymns, and songs from the Spirit. Sing and make music from your heart to the Lord. (Ephesians 5:18-19)**

Being **"filled with the Spirit"** in the context of the Scripture above is being filled with spiritual music. After all, the word "psalms" literally comes from the "Middle English, from Old English *psealm*, from Late Latin *psalmus*, from Greek *psalmos*, literally, twanging of a harp, from *psallein* to pluck, play a stringed instrument."[1]

Music is very powerful! It can be used for great good and for great evil. When we sing songs to God with all our hearts, we are filled with the Holy Spirit. If we are full of the Spirit, there is no room for sexual sin. When our minds are beginning to empty, why not fill them with music for God? This is a great way to stay pure.

We need to always have good music on our phones ready to be played when our minds can be idle and empty. I play spiritual songs when I work out. This is a great way to stay pure in the gym as the dress code, in terms of purity, leaves much to be desired!

> *Blessed is the one*
> *Who does not walk in step with the wicked*
> *Or stand in the way that sinners take*
> *Or sit in the company of mockers,*
> *But whose delight is in the law of the Lord,*
> *And who meditates on his law day and night.*
> *That person is like a tree planted by streams of water,*
> *Which yields its fruit in season*
> *And whose leaf does not wither –*
> *Whatever they do prospers. (Psalm 1:1-3)*

There is great power in meditating on God's Word day and night. The psalm above says that when we do this, we are blessed, the blessing being prospering and bearing fruit for God. This is so, because when we have God's Word in our hearts constantly, we will do His will. Implied in the passage is the fact that if we do not meditate on God's word day and night, then we will fall into wickedness.

Thinking about God's Word through the day is paramount in preventing us from having an idle mind, and therefore, it prevents Satan from attacking us with impure thoughts because our minds are empty. Psalm 119:96 reads:

> *To all perfection I see a limit, but your commands are boundless.*

This is a great verse in that it teaches us how limitless the Word of God really is. The Scriptures are *"boundless"* in the sense they have no limits. We will never get bored by them. Every time we read the Bible, the Spirit will speak to us and teach incredible things. It is the best "entertainment" in the world. God and his Word are the purpose and reason for our existence. All we need to have is the heart and the hunger to learn from God. As it says in Psalm 119:18,

> *Open my eyes that I may see wonderful things in your law.*

As with all things of God, we have to seek in order to find. We need to seek God's Word. We need to seek to learn every single day and meditate on the word both night and day, and not only will we be strong spiritually, but we will be sexually pure as well!

> *Therefore, with minds that are alert and fully sober, set your hope on the grace to be brought to you when Jesus Christ is revealed at his coming. (1 Peter 1:13)*

This is a wonderful thing! That is, to set your mind on God's grace. The *"grace to be received"* is to be with Christ in heaven and to have a continuous relationship with him without the weaknesses and temptations of this dark world. What do I mean by this? We need to think about heaven! We need to see heaven as our goal! This goal is what drives us in part because it is our reward from God for earnestly seeking him! (Hebrews 11:6) This world is wicked, twisted and evil, but in heaven it will not be like this. It will be perfect. Let us look at the Scripture in 1 John 3:2-3,

> *Dear friends, now we are children of God, and what we will be has not yet been made known. But we know that when Christ appears, we shall be like him, for we shall see him as he is. All who have this hope in him purify themselves, just as he is pure.*

This is the hope that purifies. We each need to be purified! Having the hope of being with Jesus in heaven purifies us! This purification is without a doubt spiritual. It is a purification of our whole selves. If it purifies us spiritually and without a doubt, it also purifies us physically in regards to sexual sin.

I find many good-hearted Christians are self-deceived in this particular area. They may be hard-working in making disciples and saving souls, but heaven, unfortunately, is not in their sights. They often end up "burned out" as the ministry of Jesus has its ups and downs. Sometimes, there is a lot of fruit in the ministry and sometimes very little! This can lead to sadness and self-doubt when the times are down. But our hope in heaven has no ups and downs. It is firm and secure!

There is a saying that I really like. It goes something to this affect, "Do you want to know where your heart is really at? Then, see where your mind goes when you are distracted!" Wow! This is intense. Many of us deny ourselves to do God's will in praying, reading the Bible, evangelizing, serving our brothers and sisters, and sacrificing our time. And because of this, we are rightfully tired! When we finally get a chance to relax and get a break and get distracted, our minds go to entertainment, a relationship, having fun, movies, music, food, sports, hobbies, etc. These are not bad things in and of themselves or sinful. It is not wrong to partake in these activities from time to time. But it does show where our hearts are at if this is what we "crave" for a distraction all the time. We know in our hearts if we find more joy in our hobbies than in God himself. Sometimes, it is our hobbies that we look for the most as we are really not in love with the ministry of Jesus because it is hard and has many difficulties! Please do not get down on yourself if this is the case. It is good to know the problem, so we can implement a solution. All Christians have been "there" from time to time. The solution is simple: Repent, and let heaven reign in our hearts as a main motivation.

The bottom line is that God needs to be our distraction. We can have a hobby from time to time, but a relationship with God and doing his will needs to be our highest joy, even though it is hard at times because of disappointments, persecutions, challenges and the like. The Christian life should not be a job that we "punch in and punch out" our eight hours a day and then go home and not think about anymore. No! God is our passion! God is what we are obsessed about! We love him more than life itself! Or do we? We may say that God is whom we love most. But if we look at our lives, where do we go for comfort? We gravitate to anything but him for comfort aside from an occasionally hobby, we are probably deceived. It is no surprise then that we are struggling with sexual sin!

God needs to be our anchor! The hope of heaven needs to be our anchor! It is this very anchor of hope that keeps us firm and steadfast until Jesus calls us one day to be with him in heaven!

> *We who have fled to take hold of the hope set before us may be greatly encouraged. We have this hope as an anchor for the soul, firm and secure. It enters the inner sanctuary behind the curtain, where our forerunner, Jesus, has entered on our behalf. (Hebrews 6:18-20)*

Simply stated, if we are imagining, meditating, pondering and thinking about being with Jesus in heaven, we will not be tempted as much with sexual sins because our minds are occupied and not idle. Let us make a decision to think about being with Jesus in heaven, and one day, we will surely and happily be!

Chapter 14
Wounds Of Sexual Immorality

Sexual immorality sadly runs rampant in our society today! It is almost a given or an afterthought that anyone who is "dating" or "seeing someone" will be involved in sexual immorality. Let us get a Biblical view of this sin.

If a man seduces a virgin who is not pledged to be married and sleeps with her, he must pay the bride-price, and she shall be his wife. If her father absolutely refuses to give her to him, he must still pay the bride-price for virgins. (Exodus 22:16)

Sadly, sex before marriage between two single people is extremely common today. However, the Scripture above sheds some light on how God feels about it. The first thing we noticed is that it was not punishable by death. When this sin happened, there were two options that could happen. The first one is that both of them get married. Sex is something sacred and only to be had in the confines of marriage. In this case, the man had to pay the bride-price for virgins to the father, and they would be married rather quickly. The second option is that the father refuses to give his daughter in marriage to this man. The father had authority over his daughter as she was still living in his house. In this case, the man still had to pay the bride-price for virgins to the father since the woman is no longer a virgin.

Unspoken here is the social shame that accompanies this act as most people would know. Sex before marriage was uncommon back then. It is not like now, when just about everybody is involved in it.

As we can see, sex before marriage was a very serious offense that required action and possibly a life-changing event in getting married. How different from today when singles engaged in sexual immorality without fear of God just for the sake of pleasure. How many single mothers and children without fathers have emerged from this type of action? The lack of self-control in this area destroys society from a social point of view, not to mention from a spiritual one. When we just want to have sex with our girlfriends or boyfriends or someone we just met at a party and not measure the consequences, society suffers as a result. More often than not, when we have casual sex and a girl gets pregnant, most of us are too young to assume this responsibility and thus, many children are born into single households. Children who grow up without fathers have a deep wound in their characters that affects every facet of their lives psychologically and emotionally. Only with Jesus can we overcome this wound as God is our "true" father.

Without a physical father, there is less protection on the child. The mother usually has to work more since the father is not there financially. (This is assuming that the mother will be responsible for the child or children.) Consequently, the children not only will miss the father but also the mother as she usually has to work more. This, in turn, leads these kids to be exposed to the "streets" more and usually have more of a propensity for alcohol, violence, sexual abuse, drugs, crime, sex, rape, poor academic performance, etc.

As we can see, sexual immorality does destroy society, and this is just because we want to have a little "fun." Let us consider the following Scripture:

> *Do not be deceived: Neither the sexually immoral nor idolaters nor adulterers nor men who have sex with men nor thieves nor the greedy nor drunkards nor slanderers nor swindlers will inherit the kingdom of God.*
>
> *Flee from sexual immorality. All other sins a person commits are outside the body, but whoever sins sexually, sins against their own body. Do you not know that your bodies are temples of the Holy Spirit, who is in you, whom you have received from God? You are not your own; you were bought a price. Therefore honor God with your bodies. (1 Corinthians 6:10-11, 18-20)*

The first thing that we need to understand from this Scripture is that Paul is writing to the Corinthian Church, which was composed of disciples. This letter is not addressed to non-Christians.

The first sin in the list is sexual immorality. The fact that it was listed first is not by chance. It is the sin that most people fall into when they turn away from God. Any of these sins in this list will prevent us from inheriting the kingdom of God! That means that if we are disciples, and we practice these sins, we will not make it to heaven! This is serious news. We can, indeed, lose our salvation. This is terrible!

Why is immorality so terrible in the eyes of God? It is so, because when we are immoral, we are sinning against our own body. The way to understand this is to know that our bodies are the temple of the Holy Spirit today. Every true Christian has the Holy Spirit living inside of them. In Old Testament times, God's Spirit resided in the Temple. The Temple was the place of worship! It was a most holy place. Jews went there to offer their sacrifices unto God. Also, sacrifices were offered for those who had sinned. People went to the Temple to repent of their sins, offer up prayers and to receive the forgiveness of their sins.

That means, when a Christian is immoral today, he is sinning "inside" the temple. The parallel would be to sin inside the Old Testament Temple! That would be horrible! It was a place of worship. Just imagine if someone was caught sinning inside the Temple. That person would surely be executed! Someone who has the audacity to do this shows no regard whatsoever for God.

It is the same thing today when we are immoral! When we are immoral, we sin against our own body because our body is the temple of the Holy Spirit with all the blessings and consequences that the Temple provided from a spiritual point of view. That is why we must stay away from sexual immorality at all costs! This sin has very serious spiritual consequences, not to mention physical ones.

I have often heard brothers confess to me that they have fallen into immorality. When I ask the specifics of the sin, it turns out that it was not sexual immorality but rather sexual impurity! There seems to be a confusion between sexual immorality and impurity. Let us clarify this issue.

One sin is sinning against our own body (immorality), the other is not. Now, all sin can eventually make us fall away from God if we remain unrepentant, but not all sin has the same consequences! Let us look at this Scripture in more depth.

> *Do you not know that he who unites himself with a prostitute is one with her in body? For it is said, "The two will become one flesh." But whoever is united with the Lord is one with him in spirit.*

> *Flee from sexual immorality. All other sins a person commits are outside the body, but whoever sins sexually, sins against their own body. Do you not know that your bodies are temples of the Holy Spirit, who is in you, whom you have received from God? You are not your own; you were bought at a price. Therefore, honor God with your bodies. (1 Corinthians 6:16-20)*

It is always wise to let the Bible define the Bible. Sexual

immorality is seen in the Scripture above as having sex with a prostitute. God only allows sex with our spouses. Any other type of sex is sexual immorality, whether it be with a prostitute or with a girlfriend or with a consensual adulterous relationship.

When we get married, the sexual act is the consummation of the marriage.

> *That is why a man leaves his father and mother and is united to his wife, and they become one flesh. Adam and his wife were both naked, and they felt no shame. (Genesis 2:24-25)*

Sex with our spouses implies that we have become one flesh.

> *Do you not know that he who unites himself with a prostitute is one with her in body? For it is said, "The two will become one flesh." But whoever is united with the lord is one with him in spirit. (1 Corinthians 6:17-18)*

When we have sex with someone, something spiritual happens. Becoming one flesh means becoming one in spirit. That is why the analogy in the Scripture above says that, *"whoever is united with the Lord is one with him in spirit."* When we are united with the Lord and are saved, we also become one in spirit with the Lord. A similar thing happens with anyone with whom we have sex. Sex is a very precious thing in the eyes of God because of the spiritual implications. That is why this sin has very serious consequences in the heart of any who commit it, not to mention the physical consequences, like having an unwanted pregnancy and/or sexually-transmitted diseases! We must flee from it.

The word for sexual immorality in the Greek is "pornea." It means illicit sexual intercourse as in adultery, fornication, homosexuality, lesbianism, intercourse with animals, etc. Sexual impurity is another thing altogether. There are sexual sins that do not include the sexual act itself with another person. These sins include lust, masturbation, watching pornography, and other sexual acts with another person like caressing, touching, etc. The word for impurity in the Greek is "akatharsia." It means uncleanness in a physical and moral way. It means the impurity of lustful, luxurious, profligate living as well as impure motives. Thus impurity is not just limited in sexual way, but also includes the impurity of the mind like jealousy, envy, bitterness, etc.

The reason I take time to make the distinction is because some Christians are sexually impure, yet they think they have been sexually immoral when they have not been. This can lead a brother with a weak conscience to fall away from God thinking that he was immoral. Impurity is also a serious sin that needs to be addressed. Immorality, however, is a wound that is much harder to recover from because of the hardening of the heart that occurs when we give ourselves over to this sin. After all, if I get angry with a brother, it is not right, but that is much different than shooting a brother with a gun. Let us have a sober view of ourselves and even our sin, so we can utilize the grace of God to repent of any and all sexual sin for his glory!

After all, the Bible does say:

> *Or do you show contempt for the riches of his kindness, forbearance and patience, not realizing that God's kindness is intended to lead you to repentance? (Romans 2:4)*

Chapter 15
Rebuilding After Adultery

Adultery! What an ugly word! Without a doubt, this word conjures up negative feelings in just about everyone! Sadly, it is not uncommon in today's society, and it is precisely what often happens in marriages that do not have God as their foundation. Many of us have suffered the direct or indirect consequences of this sin in some form or another in our lives. These consequences have dire effects on society as a whole, through separations, divorces, poverty and the break-up of the nuclear family, which is so vital for child-rearing. As devastating as this sin can be, with God there is hope for rebuilding. With God, there is always hope! King David, sadly, was not exempt from this sin as we see in 2 Samuel 11:1-5,

In the spring, at the time when kings go off to war, David sent Joab out with the king's men and the whole Israelite army. They destroyed the Ammonites and besieged Rabbah. But David remained in Jerusalem. One evening David got up from his bed and walked around on the roof of the palace. From the roof he saw a woman bathing. The woman was very beautiful, and David sent someone to find out about her. The man said, "She is Bathsheba, the daughter of Eliam and the wife of Uriah the Hittite." Then David sent messengers to get her. She came to him, and he slept with her. (Now she was purifying herself from her monthly uncleanness.) Then she went back home. The woman conceived and sent word to David, saying, "I am pregnant."

David was married and so was Bathsheba. In David's case, he had many wives to satisfy his sexual desires. However, the Scripture in Ecclesiastes 1:8 rings true:

The eye never has enough of seeing, nor the ear its fill of hearing.

This means that human desire is never truly satisfied. We always want more. A man can have the most attractive woman as his wife, but eventually he will desire another woman because this is the nature of human beings. David and Bathsheba did not understand this. Both of them, foolishly, gave in to their lust and were adulterous. Knowing that it was morally wrong, they still chose to satisfy the desires of the flesh. Instead of being in the battle with his fellow soldiers, David was at home resting. The once great king who *"led [Israel] in their campaigns"* (1 Samuel 18:16) was now a "comfortable" king who no longer felt the need to be on the front lines. Instead of honoring her husband who was fighting for his country, Bathsheba gave into, perhaps, her loneliness and longed for affection. What could have been a more tempting offer than the affection of a handsome and powerful king!

Sadly, David, wanted to cover up his adultery so he decides to send a letter to the commander of his army, Joab, instructing him to place Bathsheba's husband, Uriah, where the battle was fiercest so that he could be killed swiftly. 2 Samuel 11:14-18 reads,

> *In the morning David wrote a letter to Joab and sent it with Uriah. In it he wrote, "Put Uriah out in front where the fighting is fiercest. Then withdraw from him so he will be struck down and die." So, while Joab had the city under siege, he put Uriah at a place where he knew the strongest defenders were. When the men of the city came out and fought against Joab, some of the men in David's army fell; moreover, Uriah the Hittite died.*

In doing this, Bathsheba became a young widow. This allowed David to quickly marry her and pretend that the pregnancy was conceived after their marriage. David seemed to have gotten away with his plan at first. However, he did not. We cannot hide anything from God because our sin is laid bare before him. (Hebrews 4:13) Our sins will always have consequences. These consequences will be seen in this life, but most importantly in the life to come, unless we repent. David and Bathsheba did indeed suffer the consequences of their sin. Their child became ill and died! (2 Samuel 12:15-19) What is remarkable, though, is that they repented after this low point in their lives! This is seen by the fact that neither David nor Bathsheba were adulterous again, as well as the fact that the next king of Israel, Solomon, came from Bathsheba and not from any of David's other wives, demonstrating God's blessing on their repentance. (2 Samuel 12:24-25) David and Bathsheba also named one of their sons Nathan, thus honoring the very Nathan that confronted him with his sin and gave him a life-saving rebuke. (2 Samuel 5:14; 1 Samuel 12:1-14) Clearly their hearts had been transformed and they were grateful for God's discipline because it trained both of them, producing a *"harvest of righteousness and peace."* (Hebrews 12:11) Many years after David sinned, God views him as a righteous man as we can see in 1 Kings 11:6,

> *So, Solomon did evil in the eyes of the Lord; he did not follow the Lord completely, as David his father had done.*

This could only mean that David truly repented and was blessed because of it! God views us as we are today and not as our past sins dictate. In fact, God does not see us just as we are, but as who we can become through Him. If we repent as Christians, God forgives us and gives us a new start. Even adulterers can repent! God wants us to repent, and he wants to give us life. This is what is says in Ezekiel 18:27-32,

> *But if a wicked person turns away from the wickedness they have committed and does what is just and right, they will save their life. Because they consider all the offenses they have committed and turn away from them,*

that person will surely live; they will not die. Yet the Israelites say, 'The way of the Lord is not just.' Are my ways unjust, people of Israel? Is it not your ways that are unjust? "Therefore, you Israelites, I will judge each of you according to your own ways, declares the Sovereign Lord. Repent! Turn away from all your offenses; then sin will not be your downfall. Rid yourselves of all the offenses you have committed, and get a new heart and a new spirit. Why will you die, people of Israel? For I take no pleasure in the death of anyone, declares the Sovereign Lord. Repent and live!

This is an amazing passage! There is no spiritual resume in God's eyes. This is good for every single one of us. If we repent, God will forgive our sins and give us a new start. God wants us to repent and live! This truth is inspiring but it begs the question: How did David and Bathsheba rebuild their marriage and their lives after their sin? Imitating what they did to rebuild what had been broken down by sin will help anyone to spiritually recover from the sin of adultery.

Steps to Rebuilding After Adultery:

1) Take Responsibility.

This applies to both the person who committed the adultery as well as the person who the adultery was committed against. Most adulterers can blame their spouse for their behavior. We have a tendency to blame shift so we can continue our sinful behavior feeling justified. You can say things like, "Well, he/she never gives me any attention. He/She is angry all the time. He/She does not want to be with me intimately." Even if there is truth in these statements, there is never an excuse to be adulterous. All marriages go through their ups and downs, but that does not give us the right to sin. David understood this as he wrote Psalm 51:3-4 where he says:

For I know my transgression and my sin is always before me. Against you, you only, have I sinned and done what is evil in your sight; so you are right in your verdict and justified when you judge.

Ultimately, all of our sin is against God. It has nothing to do with the other person. We need to be mindful of God. We are adulterous because we do not love God. We are adulterous because we do not fear God. It is all about God. If we have a godly view of sin, we will never be adulterous and blame the other person. Our spouse never "makes" us sin. As a matter of fact, our spouse never makes us do anything. No one can make us do anything, and we must take responsibility for our actions.

Ultimately, all of our sin is against God. It has

nothing to do with the other person. We need to be mindful of God. We are adulterous because we do not love God. We are adulterous because we do not fear God. It is all about God. If we have a godly view of sin, we will never be adulterous and blame the other person. Our spouse never "makes" us sin. As a matter of fact, our spouse never makes us do anything. No one can make us do anything, and we must take responsibility for our actions.

As stated above, the person that has been sinned against needs to take responsibility as well. What could he or she have done better to prevent this? Let's say that a husband committed adultery against his wife. The wife needs to ask, "What could I have done to prevent this?" Of course, you are not responsible for the adultery, but you are responsible for your conduct and how it can affect your spouse. This can be a tough pill to swallow, but it is rare that a loved, respected and appreciated spouse will throw away that which they cherish and destroy the trust and intimacy built over the course of years simply for a random act of adultery.

Often times, there is neglect in the area of intimacy in the marriage which can "tempt" the other partner to sin. God created sex to be enjoyed in the marriage relationship. (Genesis 2:25) The frequency of the sexual intimacy should be based on the spouse who has the greater desire since their bodies belong to each other. (1 Corinthians 7:2-5) Neglect in this area can lead a spouse to be more tempted to fall into adultery. The marriage bed needs to be protected! Willfully choosing to neglect your spouse sexually is likely to plant seeds of rejection ("I am not wanted."), insecurity ("I am no longer desirable."), hopelessness ("This will never change.") and bitterness. ("I will not accept this treatment.")

Another area of neglect in the marriage is often seen at the friendship and emotional level. This can lead a partner to look for that emotional and relational intimacy with someone else, and thus, temptation for adultery can occur. Your emotions can lead to adultery even if what you were originally seeking is a friendship with the opposite sex. Your intentions may have started off as pure, but it is so crucial that you guard your heart because it can be deceitful and your emotions can lead you astray. (Proverbs 4:23; Jeremiah 17:9) Both spouses need to take responsibility of the adultery for healing to occur.

2) Forgive Each Other.

Forgiveness is essential for every disciple of Christ to make it to heaven. If we do not forgive, God will not forgive us. (Matthew 6:14-15) How could we not forgive when Christ forgave us of all of our sins? Who do we think we are? Now forgiveness does not mean that you accept the behavior, that the other partner has a license to sin, or that your partner is to be trusted immediately. Adultery is so serious that God is even willing to allow a divorce under these circumstances. Nonetheless, if both partners are willing to follow Jesus and submit to his Lordship, then any marriage can heal and rebuild its foundations with that of Christ.

Forgiveness is not easy, but with the Lord we can do it! A great place to start is to pray for your spouse every day. At first you may not want to. Even if it feels forced or unnatural, you need to deny yourself and pray for your spouse. These prayers need to be for good things for your spouse. You do not need to pray for God to humble your spouse or make them feel what you are feeling and to pay for their wrongs. God will discipline accordingly. No one gets away with sin. (Colossians 3:25) Pray for your spouse to be blessed, to love God deeply, and for God to do a miracle in his or her life. Pray for the good and not for the bad. After a while of persevering in prayer for your spouse, God will grant you a soft heart and you will be able to truly forgive. Once you forgive, it is like taking yourself out of the prison you have built. It may take you months in prayer for God to grant you a soft heart so that you can forgive, but the prayer of a righteous man and woman is *"powerful and effective."* (James 5:16)

I can only imagine that Bathsheba had to go through this in order to forgive David. After all, she did not know, initially, that David wrote a letter instructing the soldiers to stand back so

165

that her husband could be killed. Imagine what that realization must have been like! She had no knowledge of this. She mourned her husband's death. (2 Samuel 11:26) How hard it must have been for Bathsheba to find out that her late husband Uriah was killed by David who was now her husband! I am sure that she wrestled with God in prayer until she was able to forgive him. Judging by later interactions with David and her sons, she had no bitterness towards David, only love and respect. That is the power of prayer and forgiveness!

Another aspect of forgiveness, that is often overlooked, is the necessity to forgive one's self. Imagine how hard it must have been for David to forgive himself for what he had done. He murdered so that he could get what he wanted. He murdered one of his fellow "mighty men." David could have been plagued with a guilty conscience that paralyzed him from doing anything for God after this juncture. Fortunately, this was not the case. By forgiving himself he accepted God's grace to move forward and continue striving to be the best that he could be for God. We definitely need to forgive ourselves in order to move forward and do great things for God. For more on this topic, please go to Chapter 11.

3) Speak The Truth.

Sadly, adultery and lies go hand in hand. The very nature and allure of adultery has to do with deception. After all, Satan is the father of lies. To rebuild a marriage, both spouses need to be committed to telling the truth and not being deceitful anymore. Luke 8:17 says:

For there is nothing hidden that will not be disclosed, and nothing concealed that will not be known or brought out into the open.

It is futile to hide sin. Most sin will come out in the open one day and people will find out. The consequences will be far worse if the sin is revealed after you have hidden it for a time. Even if you manage to cover it your lie, it will come out at the judgement day. After a while, if you keep lying, you will start to believe the lie yourself. This is exactly what happened to David. After David's adultery, lying about Uriah's death, and having a son who was born out of the adultery with Bathsheba, David was deceived. Since the child was born, about nine months had passed. This meant that he had all this time to repent but chose not to do so. Fortunately, the prophet Nathan comes to confront David about his sin. (2 Samuel 12:1-14) Nathan tells him a story about a poor man who lost his one, precious ewe lamb to a rich man who had many lambs. Sadly, David does not have the conscience to comprehend that the story was about him (the rich man) who took precious wife of another. Only after Nathan blatantly tells David that this story was about him are his spiritual eyes reopened. David was deceived for a long time and only after he became honest with his sin was his heart healed. Thank God that he did! The same applies to us. We cannot heal unless we confess our sin. (1 John 1:8-10) Let us be open and tell the truth and let us become men and women who speak the truth because sin will come out one day whether we want it to or not. If you live by the truth you will be blessed. If you do not, you will be cursed. Duplicity will destroy you, so let us decide to live by the truth and to not lie. (Proverbs 11:3) If we do lie for some reason, let us be quick to confess and repent from it. (James 5:16)

4) Say 'No' To Sin.

David and Bathsheba were never adulterous again. They repented! That is the goal. The plan is to hate the sin and never commit it again. It hurts God, your spouse, family members, etc. To say no to adultery, you must understand the grace of God. Titus 2:11-12 says:

For the grace of God has appeared that offers salvation to all people. It teaches us to say "No" to ungodliness and worldly passions, and to live self-controlled, upright and godly lives in this present age.

The grace of God is the most powerful force in the world! It is the undeserved love of God that he gives to sinful creatures like us who do not deserve any forgiveness on our best day. God gives us his grace! What an incredible gift from God! For more on saying 'no' to sin and repenting, please go to Chapter 6 and Chapter 10, respectively

In conclusion, any marriage can heal from adultery if both spouses are willing to submit to Christ. Submitting to Christ is not something burdensome. It is something great. His yoke is light and we have heaven awaiting us one day so we can be with him for an eternity. May our marriages be used by God so we can make it to heaven and help many others to make it as well.

Chapter 16
Chivalrous Eyes

I made a covenant with my eyes
Not to look lustfully at a young woman.
(Job 33:1)

We need to "watch" our eyes! Job made a covenant with his eyes not to lust. We need to do the same to have victories over the way man looks at a women (or women looking at men). We need to view the opposite sex in a pure way and not with eyes full of lust. As men, we need to have a sense of honor and chivalry in the way we look at women.

Unfortunately, for most men, women are viewed as sexual objects. (2 Corinthians 5:16) This is very unfortunate and not godly! Many women feel that men mainly look at them for sexual reasons. Men without the Spirit give full reign to their lusts, and thus they cannot control themselves. With disciples, it is different. We indeed have the Spirit as Christians. Jesus gives us a great insight into this area with this Scripture:

> *He called a little child to him, and placed the child among them. And he said: "Truly I tell you, unless you change and become like little children, you will never enter the kingdom of heaven." (Matthew 18:2-3)*

To enter the kingdom of heaven we need to change and become like children. We need to change because as adults, we tend to see women and men incorrectly. We tend to see them with our eyes full of lust. We need to look at women (and women at men) as children do. They do so with the utmost purity. Children are not entertaining impure sexual thoughts. Children are pure by nature and are thus praised by Jesus! Women are not to be lusted after, nor are men by women, but are to be loved as precious creations of God. If they are not Christians, we need to do our best so they can be saved and come to have a relationship with Jesus.

Instead of lusting after women or women for men, we should be sharing our faith with them like Jesus did with the Samaritan woman in John 4. At the same time, because of our tendency towards lust, there are some safeguards we should implement so that we do not lust. Let us consider this Scripture:

> **Brothers and sisters, stop thinking like children. In regard to evil be infants, but in your thinking be adults. (1 Corinthians 14:20)**

We should be like children in reference to our gravitation towards sin, however like adults, in our thinking. So we let the Bible shape our thinking in this area! We already saw that sexual attraction is not sin. What happens when we are married, or dating or single, and there is a sister in the church to which we feel attracted? This will happen to everyone. It will also happen from the sisters towards the brothers as well. It is natural. This situation can happen at work or at school or at the gym or any place that we frequent and see the same women constantly. What will we do?

If we get too close to a sister or to a non-Christian woman, we will eventually lust, and there is a potential for an emotional attachment to develop. This has sadly led not a few to fall into sin.

What do we do in this situation?

1) <u>Share your faith with her if she is not a Christian</u>. This is the first step. Usually when we share our faith, even if the woman or man has a reciprocal attraction towards us, the tension subsides. If the woman had an attraction towards us, she tends to lose it, or it diminishes when we share our faith. And who knows? Maybe, one day, she will come to church and study the Bible and become a Christian. And maybe, after some growth in the Lord, a dating relationship can start or even a marriage?

   Sometimes, after we share our faith with a woman, the opposite happens. She may find us intriguing. It might make her even more attracted, since we could be perceived as a "good man." If this is the case, then we should apply the second point.

2) <u>Avoid when possible</u>. This is the general rule when we have an attraction to someone. We need to try to avoid this person without being rude to them. Eventually, they will get the drift.

If the situation happens at church in which there is a sister we feel attracted to in the fellowship but we do not want to sin against God by having lustful thoughts about her, we need to avoid her whenever possible. We can greet her in the fellowship but we should not try to carry on a long conversation with her. When we have to talk, we need to do it straight to the point and look only at her eyes. We may come off as a little distant, but that is a small price to pay to stay pure.

Let us stay pure at all costs!

Part Four
Specific Battles

Chapter 17
The Battle Of Pornography

We live in an unprecedented age, the age of unlimited information accessibility! Since we have the internet, just about anyone can have access to whatever they want online. It is just as easy as picking up our phone and searching on Google. Just about everyone has a phone or computer that can reach the internet. While this is a good thing from one perspective, from another point of view, it is very bad.

Watching pornography is easier now than ever before and a huge problem in our society today. Let us consider these statistics:

"30 percent of all data transferred across the Internet is porn. 70% of men and 30% of women watch pornography every week, and this stat is rapidly increasing every week. Larger porn sites get more visitors each month than Netflix, Amazon and Twitter combined." [1]

The sad thing is that even children are watching pornography, because it is so easily accessible. We are witnessing a generation in which, sadly, most people are watching pornography with no or very little parental control, and the effect of this on society, relationships and marriages is devastating. Most people regularly lose the battle of watching pornography! Only God can free us from this deadly vice! The Bible says in Matthew 6:22-23,

> *The eye is the lamp of the body. If your eyes are healthy, your whole body will be full of light. But if your eyes are unhealthy, your whole body will be full of darkness. If then the light within you is darkness, how great is that darkness!*

Our eyes as Christians are our spiritual lamps. If our eyes are healthy, then our body is full of light. If unhealthy, our body is full of darkness. What we allow our eyes to see determines who we are spiritually. It determines what we are full of. There are two choices: light or darkness. If we watch pornography, our bodies are full of darkness. Watching pornography leads to other sins, because we are already under the control of Satan. Masturbation and sexual immorality began to be our masters, and it can lead to adultery.

Sadly, King David fell into pornography before he fell into adultery, an unwanted pregnancy, and the murder of Bathsheba's husband.

> *One evening David got up from his bed and walked around on the roof of the palace. From the roof he saw a woman bathing. The woman was very beautiful, and David sent someone to find out about her. The man said, "She*

is Bathsheba, the daughter of Eliam and the wife of Uriah the Hittite." Then David sent messengers to get her. She came to him, and he slept with her. (Now she was purifying herself from her monthly uncleanness.) Then she went back home. The woman conceived and sent word to David, saying, "I am pregnant." (2 Samuel 11:2-5)

This is indeed a sad account, but it all started with David's eyes. Instead of being in the battle, he stayed home in his palace. It says that he got up in the evening. Getting up in the evening is a sign of spiritual laziness. It does not say that he prayed when he got up, or that he read the Holy Scriptures. When he got up, he looked from the roof of the palace where he saw, dare we saw, a pornographic scene, the naked body of Bathsheba. Maybe it was not the first time he did this. Maybe this is the reason he went to the roof. Maybe he wanted to go to the roof because of the potential of seeing women bathing from this high point. The images of Bathsheba filled his mind and body with darkness. Those images filled him with lust even though he had many wives already to satisfy his enlarged sexual desire. After all, if someone is satisfied with their first spouse, they do not need any others. As we can see, David had a huge problem with lust, but his adultery with Bathsheba could have been avoided if he took care of his eyes. He would not have been adulterous if he had not seen Bathsheba naked. He was not radical with his eyes. He allowed pornography into his life, and thus reaped horrible life-long consequences because of it.

Pornography starts with curiosity. The old saying, "Curiosity killed the cat" is indeed true. This often times is how we fall. Curiosity starts when we see a picture of a pretty lady or good-looking man with her or his clothes on. Then we want to see the person with less clothes, like a woman in a bikini or a man in his bathing suit. Then, curiosity increases and we take it a step further, looking at a man or woman who is naked. Our curiosity then leads us to watch a sexual scene and so on. Before we know it, we are hooked on pornography and receive the consequences of it. There is guilt and shame, which damage our character. There is embarrassment, which in many cases leads to lying. We hide the sin because we are embarrassed. Because we do not repent, our pornography use only increases, furthering our desire to lie more, because we do not want to get caught.

It goes without saying that this sin has an effect on our relationship with God. It is harder to pray and read the Word of God and to evangelize, because we feel like hypocrites. And unfortunately, that is exactly what we are – hypocrites!

1) <u>We need to fear God more than we fear people</u>.

Therefore confess your sins to each other so that you may be healed. The prayer of a righteous person is powerful and effective. (James 5:16)

God created confession toward one another because he knows our characters. More often than not, when we have the sin of pornography, we do not confess it to others. We do not confess because we are embarrassed about what others will think. Seldom are we embarrassed about what God thinks about our pornography. We pray to God and ask him for forgiveness, but we do not feel that badly about our sin. But when we think about confessing to others, we feel very ashamed and shrink back from the light.

The truth is that we fear people, and their reactions more than we fear God. This is precisely why God wants us to confess to each other. The *"each other"* in James, is referring to other Christians that can help us with our sin, as opposed to confessing to non-Christians who cannot help us because they are, most likely, in the same sins.

When we confess to others, we feel the guilt and shame of our sins in a good way, but something else begins to happen that is pretty amazing. Our hearts begin to heal. Only God can forgive sins, but healing starts with confessing. Our hearts begin to get soft when we open up, and we are more receptive to the word of God in this state.

2) The best cure is prevention.

The prudent see danger and take refuge, but the simple keep going and pay the penalty. (Proverbs 27:12)

Here is a radical advice: Try not to look at women! This does not mean never looking at a woman. Men have a very strong tendency to lust. The best cure is prevention. This applies not only in regards to physical diseases, but as well to spiritual ones like watching pornography.

Some watch pornography because they have been lusting constantly at work or at school during the day. Their minds are filled with lust. That lust then leads them to watch pornography when we get home.

This is my advice: Only look at women when we have to interact with them. When we do interact, only look at their eyes and never at any part of their bodies. This advice is regarding the women we have to interact with, be it at work, on campus, etc.

But when we are walking on the street, or on campus, or driving or on the subway, we should not look at women at all. Only look at them with our peripheral vision. The great thing about peripheral vision is that it sees movement but not detail. It is great that God created vision to be this way. When I see a woman walking towards me, I see it as a test from God. Why is that? Because I know myself. I can lust at almost any woman. It does not matter too much how they look. This is how lustful I know I can be as a man, and most men are the same. So, going back to the woman walking down the street. As she approaches, I do not look at her directly. I only see her peripherally, which gives me no detail at all. I see this as a small victory. I congratulate myself in this "little victory." I give a spiritual "high five" to myself in this situation. This victory builds self-esteem, which in turn will give us more victories in the future.

If our day is like this, our minds will not be full of lust, and consequently, we will not have the temptation, or we will have less temptation to watch pornography or masturbate.

3) Have an accountability partner.

This goes hand-in-hand with confessing our sins, but more so. Having an accountability partner is having a friend or mentor that is going to look out for us in this specific area. The whole point is being able to avoid the sexual sin at all just like Alcoholics Anonymous and Narcotics Anonymous have these types of supportive relationships. It is good to have someone in the church in a similar manner, who will keep an eye out for us on a daily basis as far as sexual temptation. Proverbs 14:12 says, *"There is a way that appears to be right, but in the end it leads to death."*

Oftentimes, because of our weakness in this area, we do not make the best decisions, and we put ourselves in compromising situations. If there is an area where we need advice, it is in this area. Most of us have really messed up our lives because of sexual sin and need advice! Our accountability partner (discipler) can give us wise advice, like putting filters on our computer and phone, so we do not watch pornography. He can ask if we did it and hold us accountable. An example of the advice we can receive would be not to go on our computer when we are alone. If we go on our computer when other people are around, it will help us avoid the temptation of watching pornography.

We can also receive the advice to avoid social media, altogether, for a while to keep us away from temptation. Another piece of good advice is to call or text our accountability partner when we feel tempted to watch pornography. God has created relationships in his church so we can help each other make it to heaven! We need to take advantage of them! Also, be someone else's accountability partner! Remember: You can't keep your purity unless you help others keep theirs.

Consider these Scriptures:

> *Listen to advice and accept discipline, and at the end you will be counted among the wise. (Proverbs 19:20)*

> *The way of fools seems right to them, but the wise listen to advice. (Proverbs 12:15)*

Surely you need guidance to wage war, and victory is won through many advisers. (Proverbs 24:6)

4) Eliminate anything that hinders.

Therefore, since we are surrounded by such a great cloud of witnesses, let us throw off everything that hinders and the sin that so easily entangles. And let us run with perseverance the race marked out for us, fixing our eyes on Jesus. (Hebrews 12:1-2)

This is an amazing Scripture that teaches us two important things. The obvious one is that we need to avoid the sin that entangles. This has been discussed in the previous three points above. But the Scripture also points out that we have to *"throw off everything that hinders."*

Everything that hinders is not sin per se, but things that which could lead to sin if left unchecked! For example, if we are not winning souls to Christ by making disciples, we are being lazy and have too much time on our hands to sin. Too much time hinders us and leads us to pornography because we are being lazy.

Another thing that can hinder us is the opposite. We can be so busy at work and school that we do not have time for God and his mission. When we are so busy and do not have time to breathe, we look for comfort, and that is when some go to pornography for that comfort. Our comfort needs to be God. In that case, we need to make time for God by cutting other things from our schedule.

In conclusion, the battle against pornography is not easy, but it is a battle that can and will be won if we follow these four points. May God guide us and give us the victory that can only be won through him!

Chapter 18
The Battle Of Masturbation

Masturbation has always been a hot topic among religious circles. Many doctors and health professionals believe that masturbation is a good thing to do. They believe it is healthy! A plethora of psychologists believe that it is good for us mentally. Many in religious circles do not believe that masturbation is sin. Many believe that it is not sin because it is better than the alternative, which is sexual immorality. They think that if we masturbate, we are satisfying ourselves sexually and thus not sinning with sexual immorality. Others say that masturbation is not a sin because the Bible does not mention it at all. If it is not in the Bible, it surely cannot be sin. Other religious people believe that masturbation is sin if we are having lustful thoughts while doing it as lustful thoughts are sinful according to Matthew 5:27-33. But the fact that we masturbate and get an organism is not sin because they are not specifically mentioned in the Bible.

How can we view masturbation in light of the Scriptures.

There are three reasons why masturbation is wrong:

That is why a man leaves his father and mother and is united to his wife, and they become one flesh. Adam and his wife were both naked, and they felt no shame. (Genesis 2:24-25)

1) Masturbation is a sexual act that God did not intend!

We see in the Scripture above what sex was all about. Sex was intended for married couples. In this type of union, there was no shame at all. After all, masturbation is having sex with ourselves. The "sex" of which God approves is within a trusting marriage relationship. Any sexual activity outside of the marriage bond is sin. According to the Scripture above, only after the marriage union can we be involved in sex and only then with only our spouse.

2) Only those who become like children enter the kingdom of heaven

He called a little child to him, and placed the child among them. And he said: "Truly I tell you, unless you change and become like little children, you will never enter the kingdom of heaven." (Luke 18:15-17)

Brothers and sisters, stop thinking like children. In regard to evil be infants, but in your thinking be adults. (1 Corinthians 14:20)

To ultimately make it to heaven, we have to become like a child. Children are sexually pure by nature! This is awesome. They are pure unless, unfortunately, they have been sexually abused.

The thought of masturbating or watching pornography does not cross a child's mind. Masturbation is wrong because children would not do it, and we have to become like a child, in regards to sin, to enter the kingdom of heaven.

3) Jesus would not masturbate; therefore, neither should we.

   Therefore, be imitators of God, as beloved children. (Ephesians 5:1 NASB)

   Our goal in life as Christians is to be like Jesus! We want to be more and more like Jesus until the day that he finally calls us to be with him. Therefore, we try to imitate God! As imitators of God, we have to ask ourselves a question. Would Jesus masturbate? Obviously, the answer is a resounding "no." So, if Jesus would not masturbate, should we? Of course not! Why not masturbate? We should not masturbate because Jesus would not do it. It does not matter what people say or even what religious leaders say. We just need to imitate Jesus' example. If we do, we will win the battle of masturbation.

Chapter 19
The Battle Of Homosexuality

If there is a controversial or urgent issue that is affecting the church today, it is how we view and deal with homosexuality!

A while back, I read an excellent book that helped shape my thinking on this very pertinent issue to our times. It is called, *Caring Beyond the Margins. What Every Christian Needs To Know About Homosexuality* by Guy Hammond who happens to be a church leader. It is an excellent book, and I strongly recommend it for anyone who wants a better understanding of this very important issue. Most of the material in this chapter has been inspired by Hammond's book.

The novel concept that I learned was that there is a difference between same-gender attraction and homosexuality. Many believe that if we are attracted to the same gender, we are homosexual, even if we have not committed any homosexual acts. There is a major difference between same-gender attraction and homosexuality.

This is what Guy Hammond wrote,

> *I am not gay, but I am same-gender attracted. It is for this reason that I do not consider myself to be a homosexual or gay; I do not live like a person who actively engages in homosexual*

relationships. This is not my identity, and therefore I am not a homosexual. I do, however, live with unwanted same-gender attractions, though I have committed myself to not entertain those appetites. I have chosen to walk along another path as I strive to follow Jesus. This is a decision that I make every day. Colossians 4:5-6 tells us, "Be wise in the way you act toward outsiders; make the most of every opportunity. Let your conversation be always full of grace, seasoned with salt, so that you may know how to answer everyone." So the words we use matter. [1]

We learn something here. Homosexual activity is always sinful. There is no excuse for this sin. However, attraction to the same gender is not sin. But how can this be true? Well, let us think about other attractions in general, for example heterosexual attraction. I may feel attracted to other women, even though I am married. I have not sinned because I am attracted to other women. The sin would be if I entertain lustful thoughts, or if I flirt with other women or masturbate thinking about them. The fact that I am attracted is not sin. It is just attraction. It is a pull due to my sinful nature, but I have not sinned by simply being attracted. I am just being tempted. (James 1:13-15)

For example, if we are attracted or pulled towards materialism, are we in sin? If we want the new car, even though we do not need it, and it would put us into debt and our current car is in perfect working order –

have we sinned? I do not think so. The fact that we are attracted towards getting that new car is not sin. We may have wanted this new car because we always liked cars and always wanted to have a car of the current year. Have we sinned by wanting this? We have not, and if we deny ourselves, it is, in fact, a victory, because although we were attracted to that new car, we did not get it. We denied ourselves. We are becoming like Jesus, building character because of this struggle. Yet we did indeed feel the attraction.

Let us take, for example, the attraction to food. If we are overweight because of pure lack of self-discipline, it is a difficult situation to be in. As we get older, our metabolism does indeed slow down for most of us, and if we eat the same as when we were younger, we will gain undesirable weight. Now, if we are tempted to overeat or attracted to certain types of foods that are unhealthy, have we sinned? We have not. And again, if we deny ourselves, we have gained an incredible victory over our temptation, and we will build our character.

Now, imagine that we are overweight, and we are attracted, or dare we say tempted, to eat a bag of chocolate chip cookies. We can feel guilty and down because we feel this way. We feel defeated, and we believe that we will never change. After all, we are overweight. What do we do next? We give in to our attraction or temptation, to cookies in this case, and we eat the whole bag. Now, we are reinforcing the fact that we will never change and that it is useless to lose weight. This over-eating, overweight self becomes our new reality, but if we are disciples walking in the light,

God does not view us in this way!

It is the same thing with same-gender attraction. The sin is not the attraction. The sin is giving in to the attraction and committing the sin. Many who practice homosexuality believe they cannot change because they feel the pull is too strong. Well, it is – without the help of God's Holy Spirit. The pull is strong with any sin that we have decided to indulge in. The fact that we are same-gender attracted is not sin. Most likely, we will have this attraction for the rest of our lives. That is ok. It is just an attraction. All Christians will face attractions and temptations in different areas for the rest of our lives because we are in the flesh.

We can live a fulfilling Christian life and be same-gender attracted!

After all, Jesus was tempted in every way but was without sin.

> *For we do not have a high priest who is unable to empathize with our weaknesses, but we have one who has been tempted in every way, just as we are – yet he did not sin. Let us then approach God's throne of grace with confidence, so that we may receive mercy and find grace to help us in our time of need. (Hebrews 4:15-16)*

> *Because he himself suffered when he was tempted, he is able to help those who are being tempted. (Hebrews*

If he was tempted in every way, and if he can help us in our time of need, that means that at least at one point in his earthly existence, he was attracted or tempted with a homosexual thought. Notwithstanding, he did not ever give in to it!

Guy Hammond also goes to list four principles for his book.

1) While living a life of active homosexuality is sinful (Leviticus 18:22, 20:13; Romans 1:26-27; 1 Corinthians 6:9-10), simply being attracted to the same gender is not.

2) The primary goal for the same-sex attracted disciple of Jesus is not to be heterosexually attracted, but to live a life of holiness while also living with same-sex attractions.

3) God is not ashamed or embarrassed of same-sex attracted Christians. Their value and worth to him and his church are not based on that criterion.

4) Every same-sex attracted follower of Jesus can absolutely live a successful Christian life that God would be incredibly proud of, whether or not their homoerotic appealing ever disappears. [2]

So, without a doubt, anyone who is homosexual can repent and live a life that pleases God. Having said that, what brings us to God's kingdom can be the very thing that takes us away from the kingdom in time. This definitely applies to homosexuality. Many come to the church and study the Bible and become disciples because they have seen the devastation that this sin has caused in their lives. When a former homosexual gets converted, they are usually a very fired up disciple due to the level of gratitude in their hearts. God has given them victory over this sin that seemed impossible to overcome in the past.

However, we need to consider this Scripture to understand what can happen to disciples after time passes.

> *When an impure spirit comes out of a person, it goes through arid places seeking rest and does not find it. Then it says, "I will return to the house I left." When it arrives, it finds the house swept clean and put in order. Then it goes and takes seven other spirits more wicked than itself, and they go in and live there. And the final condition of that person is worse than the first. (Luke 11:24-26)*

The evil spirit always wants to come back and harm and possess the person whom it had in its grips before. As stated above, this spirit does not come alone but seeks help from other spirits that are even more wicked. Those other spirits can often be in the form of guilt, embarrassment, shame and frustration. And this is where many of our brothers and sisters that are same-gender attracted fail. When they are first converted, they are sure that our lives have completely changed, and they have – God says we are new creations. (2 Corinthians 5:16-17) Yet, after a time in the Kingdom, they begin to be tempted and attracted to the same sex again, just like before they were baptized. Yet they may have expected not to be tempted or attracted to the same sex ever again. After all, we are Christians and have prayed fervently to God to take this attraction away. If the attraction persists, it seems like God is not answering the prayer because we are still attracted to the same sex. That is where guilt, embarrassment, shame and frustration kick in. We feel guilty that we are still attracted to the same-gender. We believe that we are in sin, and perhaps even good-intentioned brothers and sisters have given us advice to pray to be attracted to the opposite sex. We may have prayed, but we are still same-gender attracted.

We are embarrassed that we are not like the rest of the fellowship. We are frustrated with our future in the kingdom. We may say things like, "How will I ever date and get married." And maybe we have taken it further than just being attracted to the same gender. Maybe we have masturbated or watched pornography, or flirted at work or had a homosexual encounter. This shame leads many to fall away from God thinking that they "never truly changed" nor will they ever truly change. Sometimes, it leads them not to believe in God or the Bible thinking that God is unfair giving us a challenge we cannot overcome. The extreme of this thinking leads to choosing to believe God must not exist or doubting that he does.

Incredibly, all this can happen because they do not understand that same-gender attraction is not sin. The sin of homosexuality is sin, but being same-gender attracted is not. I have noticed that once I have explained this to the brothers, there is a great sense of relief and peace that comes their way. Many have said that it feels like a huge weight has been lifted from their backs. They feel free! They feel sane! They know that Satan no longer has a grip on their weak consciences. As the Scripture says, *"The truth will set us free."* And now, they have the tools to overcome, because they can deal with their same sex attraction in a healthy way, and show this wicked world that God can overcome any and all obstacles through the grace and truth available to us throughout the precious blood of Jesus!

In conclusion, same-gender attracted disciples may feel they have a harder time as disciples of Jesus because of the constant temptation. However, is not it the same for any disciple that wants to live the Christian life regardless of their set of temptations? Satan goes after everyone who is a disciple of Jesus. Understanding that same-gender attraction is not sin frees us from a deceived mindset which, in turn, will give us the "way out" to live a righteous life.

After all, God promises that in 1 Corinthians 10:13,

No temptation has overtaken you except what is common to mankind. And God is faithful; he will not let you be tempted beyond what you can bear. But when you are tempted, he will also provide a way out so that you can endure it.

Chapter 20
The Battle Of Sexual Dreams

We all dream when we sleep. Sometimes we remember our dreams and sometimes we do not. What about sexual dreams? Have we sinned when we have a sexual dream? After all, we are not in control when we dream. This is an important question as most men have sexual dreams and sometimes women do as well. Often, these sexual dreams are accompanied by an ejaculation and/or an orgasm. Some feel very guilty and defeated when this happens, and it can lead to a downward spiral of masturbation and pornography.

As a young Christian, I started having nocturnal emissions, and often sexual dreams accompanied these emissions. Because I became a Christian, I had stopped masturbating and having sex. What a victory! But when this started happening, I became alarmed! Had I sinned? I felt guilty and ashamed! What was I to do? I prayed to God, and I confessed this to other brothers.

I asked one particular brother about this and he referred to Genesis 38:8-10, which reads:

> *Then Judah said to Onan, "Sleep with your brother's wife and fulfil your duty to her as a brother-in-law to raise up offspring for your brother." But Onan knew that the child would not be his; so whenever he slept with his brother's wife, he spilled his semen on the*

ground to keep from providing offspring for his brother. What he did was wicked in the Lord's sight; so the Lord put him to death also.

This brother told me that Onan wasted his seed (sperm) and thus he sinned. Our seed was only to be used for our wife. God killed him because of this. So he told me that indeed I had sinned because I had not used my "seed" with my wife. This was confusing because I was single at the time. So, I talked to other brothers, and then I looked more carefully at the Scripture above and discovered that it did not teach that at all. It taught something else.

Onan was not killed for wasting his seed per se. He was killed because he did not want to give his sister-in-law children because his brother had died. In verses 8-9, it reads:

Then Judah said to Onan, "Sleep with your brother's wife and fulfil your duty to her as a brother-in-law to raise up offspring for your brother." But Onan knew that the child would not be his.

As it turns out, it was not a sexual issue at all. It was a selfishness issue since the children with her would carry his brother's name and not his! God killed him because of his selfishness. This gave me some comfort. We need to understand that nocturnal emissions are normal in men that are nohaving sex or masturbating. Nocturnal emissions that happen to disciples can be weird because we never or almost never had them

196

before we were Christians. Why is that? Because most of us masturbated so much that the body never had a need to do that.

Now that we have become new creations, this phenomenon can occur. We need to understand that if we are not ejaculating, our body needs to secrete the semen it produces from our body. There are two ways the body does this. One is by nocturnal emission, which can happen once a week or so, or once every two weeks, or even more interspaced. We wake up in the morning and secreted semen in our underwear.

We have not sinned if this happens!

The other way the body secretes semen is gradually every day. We will see some semen when we urinate and this is completely normal. We have not sinned when this happens either. We need not feel guilty or shame about it. It should actually be a victory, since we have changed our lives. Only God with the Holy Spirit has the power to do this.

Now, what about the sexual dream itself? Is it sin when we have a sexual dream? The answer is no! There is no Scripture that says that having a sexual dream is sin. There is a Scripture we must consider. It is in Job 33:14-18,

> *For God does speak – now one way, now another –*
> *though no one perceives it.*
> *In a dream, in a vision of the night,*
> *when deep sleep falls on people*

as they slumber in their beds,
he may speak in their ears
and terrify them with warnings,
to turn them from wrongdoing
and keep them from pride,
to preserve them from the pit,
their lives from perishing by the sword.

This is a great Scripture! It teaches that God speaks to us, although we do not perceive him speaking. The example here is that he can speak to us in a dream so as to warn us! There have been times when I have had a sexual dream, and then I finally wake up. The first thing I do is pray to God, and thank him that it was just a dream! The dream thus becomes a warning from God so that we will not sin in the future.

I have found that when brothers are sinning during the day with many lustful thoughts, especially if they are not openly confessing and renouncing their lust, this can in turn lead to having sexual dreams because it is, unfortunately, in their minds a lot. The lustful thoughts may trigger the unconscious mind as it dreams. Having said that, I do believe that there are many times that we can have sexual dreams without having lusted during the day.

Furthermore, I believe that Satan tries to utilize these sexual dreams so we feel defeated, and then we are easier to lead into sin while we are awake. At the same time, I believe that God is utilizing these dreams to warn us, so we will have convictions on being pure. In every event in life, both Satan and God are working in the same time. Satan is ultimately working to destroy us, and God is ultimately working to save us and make us more like Jesus. It is up to us to choose what we do in any and every event. Sexual dreams are no different! How we are going to see them and react to them is up to us. Let's not be over-guilty and weakened by Satan, but rather allow God to use sexual dreams to draw us near to him and make us more pure for him!

Chapter 21
The Battle Of The Ticking
Biological Clock Of Women

There is a segment of single women I have seen that have a hard time staying faithful if they do not date and eventually marry. That is why Paul encourages the young "widows" to marry and have children. A widow has had the misfortune of her husband dying. Widows in a first century context can correlate to single women in the church, today, because they do not have husbands. As it says in 1 Timothy 5:11-12, 14-15,

> *As for younger widows, do not put them on such a list. For when their sensual desires overcome their dedication to Christ, they want to marry. Thus they bring judgement on themselves, because they have broken their first pledge.*
>
> *So I counsel younger widows to marry, to have children, to manage their homes and to give the enemy no opportunity for slander. Some have in fact already turned away to follow Satan.*

In the first century, it was very rare to have single women, unlike today. Most women back then married extremely early in contrast to today's cultural standards. A lot of women now marry well into their thirties after finishing their university studies and other endeavors. Thus, a considerable number of the single women converted today are in their late 20's and early 30's and beyond. Since they are single when they enter into the kingdom, it is hard for these women to stay faithful because their biological clock is ticking, and subsequently, many do not have the patience to wait for a godly, pure man as they want to date and marry quickly.

Most women understand that after a certain age, it is dangerous to have kids, as well, some women have pressure from their families to get married. These pressures lead some to fall away from God and look to date and marry a man "in the world." Sadly, these men do not have the standards of purity and a reverent fear of God because they are not disciples of Jesus.

This pressure leads many of them to be immoral just to achieve their dream of getting married. It is sad as they fall away, and God may indeed give them their man and children. But sadly, more often than not, these women have "bad" marriages that seem to be a nightmare and many end up in divorce. God's way is the only way that works. As it says in Matthew 7:24-27,

> *Therefore everyone who hears these words of mine and puts them into practice is like a wise man who built his house on the rock. The rain came down, the streams rose, and the winds blew and beat against that house; yet it did not fall, because it had its foundation on the rock. But everyone*

who hears these words of mine and does not put them into practice is like a foolish man who built his house on sand. The rain came down, the streams rose, and the winds blew and beat against that house, and it fell with a great crash.

The only foundation we can have for our lives that works is Jesus Christ and his Word. As Christians, we need to date and marry only other Christians, as it says in 1 Corinthians 7:39,

A woman is bound to her husband as long as he lives. But if her husband dies, she is free to marry anyone she wishes, but he must belong to the Lord.

This is a hard teaching, yet it is the only way we can ensure a godly marriage and making it to heaven as well. It is God's plan for a Christian woman to marry a godly husband and for a Christian man to marry a godly woman. Anything else will fail to please God. It is better to stay single than to marry someone outside the faith.

I totally believe that most Christians should marry one day, as it says in 1 Corinthians 7:9,

But if they cannot control themselves, they should marry, for it is better to marry than to burn with passion.

A Christian marriage is a great way to control our

sexual passions in the way that God intended. However, there are some Christians that will not marry, although these brothers and sisters are surely in the minority. Our Lord Jesus speaks about this in Matthew 27:11-12,

> *Jesus replied, "Not everyone can accept this word, but only those to whom it has been given. For there are eunuchs who were born that way, and there are eunuchs who have been made eunuchs by others – and there are those who choose to live like eunuchs for the sake of the kingdom of heaven. The one who can accept this should accept it."*

There are three categories of people that will not marry:

1) They cannot have sex for a biological reason.
2) They have unfortunately been castrated by others.
3) They choose to stay single to serve God.

This means that Jesus was a eunuch because he decided not to marry to serve God's kingdom.

Women reaching their age limit in child-bearing must trust in the Lord in prayer and look for a godly Christian man, not settling for Satan's lie of marrying a non-Christian husband who in turn may make their lives worse. Most important to never forget, they will be eternally separated from God! Let us trust the Lord in this area!

Chapter 22
The Battle For A Godly Marriage

He who finds a wife finds what is good and receives favor from the Lord. (Proverbs 18:2)

Marriage is something incredible that God created for the majority of men and women in the world. It is *"finding favor from the Lord"* when we find a spouse!

The Bible also says in Genesis 2:24-25,

That is why a man leaves his father and mother and is united to his wife, and they become one flesh. Adam and his wife were both naked, and they felt no shame.

This amazing Scripture helps us understand Biblical marriage. The first marriage was before the fall of man in which Adam and Eve ate the forbidden fruit. Why is that significant? Because the marriage union between a man and woman was instituted by God before sin came into the world. Marriage was all along God's idea and not man's. How sad it is when couples get together and have children and do not get married. It is not surprising that couples who just live together are more likely to separate than married couples.

That is not to say that most marriages are in good shape. Unfortunately, most marriages are not based on the Holy Scriptures and thus end in separation and divorce at alarming rates. Or, they may stay together and yet be "emotionally divorced." However, the problem here is not the godly institution of marriage but sin. Only when we apply the principles of the Scriptures, will our marriages truly work. Usually, those principles are opposite to what a man desires in his flesh.

One common problem in marriage has to do with sexual purity. Some single brothers believe that marriage is the solution to their constant impurity, meaning that when they are married they will not struggle anymore. This is far from the truth, unfortunately. Sometimes we can have more sexual temptation being married than being single. It has to do with our mindset. The single mindset versus the married mindset in regards to sexual temptation is somewhat different. The single mind just shuts off anything that has to do with sexuality as a whole, so as not to sin. For the married, he does not because he is having sex with his wife. In this way, he is open sexually. Thus, from a certain point of view, it is harder sometimes for the married brother to stay pure than for the single brother. Let me explain.

For example, what if the wife cannot have sex for a certain reason. Maybe it is a health reason like an operation, travelling or even a fight. The married brother has an expectation of frequent sex, and when it does not happen, the temptation can be harder than that of a single brother, because the single brother just shuts off anything and everything sexual.

This is especially true when the wife does not want to have sex for some reason. Sadly, I have seen married brothers fall into masturbation or pornography when this specific scenario occurs. The sole solution for purity is not marriage. It is our relationship with God! Having said that, when our marriage is going well, it will be a great safeguard in our purity because both of the spouses are seeking God, they can easily fix whatever happens in their relationship. A marriage in the kingdom is awesome and one of the greatest gifts God can give while we are here on earth.

Another problem arises in marriage because of the expectation that we have of our spouse. Most want to get married because they want the other person for companionship to make them happy. This is a recipe for disaster! The main purpose of marriage is to help each other make it to heaven! When we make our spouse the center of our happiness, the relationship will "go all wrong" because in essence, the spouse becomes our idol. Only God can make us happy! As it says in Psalm 119:1-2,

> **Blessed are those whose ways are blameless,**
> **who walk according to the law of the Lord.**
> **Blessed are those who keeps his statutes**
> **and seek him with all their heart.**

True happiness is a by-product of seeking God. No man or woman has the capacity to make us happy all the time. It is unfair to put that expectation on the spouse, but that is precisely what we tend do. Then, our world comes crashing down because we realize that the other person is not perfect, but rather a sinner. Thus, the person that we loved the most on the planet when we went to the altar and were married, more often than not becomes the person we resent the most, and in some cases hate the most in this world.

In my opinion, marriage can be defined in one word: Giving! Marriage is all about giving unconditionally to our spouse and expecting nothing in return. This is being like Jesus! Do we want our spouse to change something? Then, we change first. If we change, maybe our spouse will change, but it is not a guarantee. That said, if we are changing to please God then he guarantees us we will be blessed! The more we give in our marriage, the more we will receive! As it says in Proverbs 11:25,

> *A generous person will prosper;*
> *whoever refreshes others will be*
> *refreshed.*

This proverb does not only apply to us giving financially, but in giving in general. If we give to our spouse, we have a much greater chance of them changing than by simply telling them that they need to change. This is why the only marriage that ultimately works is the Christian marriage! Why? We each love God more than our spouse. If the husband loves God more than his wife, then he will be patient with her in her shortcomings and will be able to forgive her when she sins. Why? He realizes that he is also a sinner, and that he falls short in many areas as well.

I cannot overstate how important forgiveness is in a marriage. It is huge! When we join two sinners in marriage, what are we going to get? More sin! Forgiveness is an issue of salvation!

> *For if you forgive other people when they sin against you, your heavenly Father will also forgive you. But if you do not forgive others their sins, your Father will not forgive your sins. (Matthew 6:14-15)*

Many marriages end in divorce over this issue. Our spouse sins against us, and we remain bitter! Bitterness is like drinking poison and wanting someone else to die! It is basically a lack of forgiveness! It is ugly! Yet, it is very common. Sadly, most non-Christian marriages that do end up staying together have bitterness in their relationship. They may smile on the outside when together. They may even be deceived and say everything is fine with their relationship, but deep down, they are trapped and confined in their own jail of bitterness. Only as disciples, can we truly forgive from the heart! We do not forgive because we do not deserve it or because the other person has changed, but because Christ forgave us of our sins. We also forgive because if we do not, we will go to hell. Therefore, we have a holy fear of our God, so we can make it to heaven! Let us forgive our spouses from the heart and let us live an incredible Christian life and enjoy great Christian marriages.

Marriage is awesome! It was meant to be awesome by

God! God's plan is for a man and a woman to be united in holy matrimony and glorify God. Unfortunately, before I was a Christian, I masturbated, watched pornography and had sex with my girlfriend. I was definitely not following God, although I deceived myself into thinking that I was, since I was going to church and reading the Bible from time to time. Yet, when I became a disciple of Jesus, everything changed. It was the very fact that I was immoral that broke me of my religious pride and come to grips that I was not a true Christian. The Word of God is powerful and effective. It really made a difference in my life. Miraculously, I stopped masturbating and watching pornography, where in the past I could not go even a week without it. I stopped having sex at the age of 22 when I was converted as a college student. By the grace of God, I was married to the woman of my dreams in Lynda. That was at age 27. That means that for five years I was totally pure. Yes, I struggled with lustful thoughts, but I did not watch pornography or masturbate during that time. By God's grace, my dating relationship with Lynda was pure. We did not have sex or touch one another lustfully. It was a total victory to the power of God and his Holy Spirit.

> *Don't you know that when you offer yourselves to someone as obedient slaves, you are slaves of the one you obey – whether you are slaves to sin, which leads to death, or to obedience, which leads to righteousness? But thanks be to God that, though you used to be slaves to sin, you have come to obey from your heart the pattern of*

teaching that has now claimed your allegiance. You have been set free from sin and have become slaves to righteousness. (Romans 6:16-18)

One very good way to overcome marital sin is by discipling! What is discipling? Discipling is helping our brothers and sisters become more and more like Jesus! It is part of the great commission that Jesus talked about in Matthew 28:19-20,

Therefore go and make disciples of all nations, baptizing them in the name of the Father and of the Son and of the Holy Spirit, and teaching them to obey everything I have commanded you. And surely I am with you always, to the very end of the age.

Jesus commands every true Christian to make disciples of all nations and then baptize them. But it does not end there. After baptism, we are to teach the young disciple of Jesus to obey Jesus's words. This is discipling! It is helping our fellow brothers and sisters to be more and more like Jesus. One of the areas in which we need the most help is in our sexual purity. We need brothers and sisters to get into our lives with the Scriptures and with godly and loving accountability to keep us pure. This is true love as we truly are our *"brothers' keeper."* (Genesis 4:9)

God works through other people to keep us close to Him in the area of sexual purity. I recommend that a brother or sister becomes our same gender accountability partner and that every night we talk about how sexual purity went that day. How did it go with our sexual thoughts? Did we flirt at work? How is it going with masturbation and pornography? Daily confession is essential for us to overcome the evil one. There is an incomplete doctrine in the religious world that teaches us only to confess to God, and that we do not need to confess to man. However, the Bible says in James 5:16,

> **Therefore, confess your sins to each other and pray for each other so that you may be healed.**

Most people do not realize that this Scripture is in the Bible. There are also other Scriptures similar to this one. Why does God want us to confess to each other. For more on confession please refer to pages 82-83.

As we can see, it is very possible to live a pure sexual life with Jesus! All we have to do is follow these simple principles and we will see our lives transformed by Christ! This is exactly what happened to me when I became a true Christian. God blessed me with an awesome marriage because of this. When Lynda, my wife, came down the aisle in a beautiful white dress, it was not only white physically, but spiritually as well. As of this writing, we have been married 15 years and we have two wonderful children that God has given us: Felipe (15) and Bella (10). The best news is that we are not an isolated case. I have seen many that have applied these principles of purity, and have seen them to go on to have great dating relationships and then great marriages. All this is to glorify God!

Chapter 23
The Battle Of Finding A Godly Dating Relationship

In our Western society, we "date" before we our married. We date someone we "like." Then, when the relationship becomes more serious and believe we have found "the one," we get engaged. After some time being engaged, we get married.

In the Bible, we do not see dating relationships. This has to do with the eastern culture. For the most part, in Biblical times and places, people were married in their early teens. The parents were the ones who chose the spouse. Thus, there was no dating back then or any need for it. If someone went on a date as we do today, this would be seen as improper and somewhat immoral. We cannot forget that the Israelite culture is an eastern culture.

Even today, cultures in the east are very different. In our churches in India, for example, single brothers and sisters do not go on dates. It is viewed as improper. In those churches, brothers and sisters get engaged directly after seeking advice from their church leaders and their parents.

I remember talking to two couples from Chennai, India whose marriages had been arranged. I asked them how they accepted not being able to choose their husband or wife. I expected them to tell me how hard it was for them to accept this restriction, and how they accepted it as their "cross to bear" when they became Christians.

However, that was not the case for either couple. Both couples told me that they were happily married and that they were grateful that people cared for them enough to find them a husband or wife! I was flabbergasted, to say the least. They both told me that they were very happy in their marriages, and that they did not agree with the Western practice of dating, which in India is seen in a negative light.

The higher rate of divorce and separation in the Western world would seem to support their ideas. Why are those marriages in India successful? They understand that love in a relationship is a decision and not a feeling! Once we make the decision to love, then good feelings and positive emotions will follow that decision.

In 1 Corinthians 13:4-8 we read:

> *Love is patient, love is kind. It does not envy, it does not boast, it is not proud. It does not dishonor others, it is not self-seeking, it is not easily angered, it keeps no record of wrongs. Love does not delight in evil but rejoices in the truth. It always protects, always trusts, always hopes, always perseveres. Love never fails.*

What an amazing Scripture! Here, we see what love is all about. There is a common denominator in most of the qualities listed. To display love and obey this commandment, we have to deny ourselves and go against our feelings. That is why love is primarily a decision. There are three words for "love" in the Greek.

1) Eros – Sexual
2) Phileo – Brotherly love
3) Agape – Self-sacrificing love

In 1 Corinthians 13: 4-8 the world love is agape not eros! This is why so many marriages fail. They believe that love is a sexual felling and not the command of a self-sacrificing love.

The first quality of love listed in 1 Corinthians 13 is *"patience."* In our sinful nature, we are not patient, and our lack of patience can be seen especially in our close relationships, where we are less on our guard and where "familiarity breeds contempt." However, in order to truly show love to our spouse, we have to be patient. To be patient with our spouse requires us to deny ourselves, especially the emotions that drive us to be impatient. We decide to be patient, even though we do not necessarily feel like being patient at first. After a while of practicing this command of love by denying ourselves and being patient with our spouse, it becomes easier as patience has now become our character. We even want to be patient because we want to love our spouse. Nevertheless, denial of self is a crucial ingredient of love. That is why to "agape" to love is a decision and not a feeling.

However, most of us do live in the Western world and expect to date before getting married. If we are faithful Christians, how does each of us find a godly spouse? First, we have to find a godly boyfriend or girlfriend. This can be a great test for most single people. People in the Bible were married early, whereas in our Western culture, people are getting married progressively later in life. Many today want to establish their careers and be "settled" before they tie the knot. This can really hurt many Christians in the church because they have the desire to get married but cannot because they either do not seem to find someone ideal, or they are not in a financial position to marry.

There are some things we can do in order to find a godly spouse:

1) <u>Persevere in prayer for God to grant you one.</u>

There are a few Scriptures to consider here. The first is James 4:2, which states, *"You do not have because you do not ask God."* This may seem obvious but it is not. Sometimes, we do not receive because we are not asking God. Sometimes we are lazy and do not pray. We simply forget. Other times, we do not pray because we do not believe that God will answer the prayer of giving us a spouse. There are also times that we do not pray because we are bitter at God, perhaps because he has not yet granted us a spouse. This is often the case if we have been in the kingdom for years but are still single. Yet, this is precisely the reason why we need to persevere in prayer. God does indeed listen to our prayers.

Another problem is that often our prayers are not consistent. We might not pray every day to God for what we want. God likes us to persevere in prayer. The Parable of the PersistentWwidow shows us this great principle. The Bible says, *"Then Jesus told his disciples a parable to show them that they should always pray and not give up."* (Luke 18:1) If God says we should always pray and never give up, he means it. We should take him at his word. God wants to see spiritual fortitude in us. Remember the words of Isaiah the prophet in Isaiah 62:6-7,

> *You who call on the Lord,*
> *give yourselves no rest,*
> *and give him no rest till he establishes*
> *Jerusalem*
> *and makes her the praise of the earth.*

God does not need rest! That is why he is God. He does not get tired of listening to all of the prayers of the world at the same time. He has no human limitations. He is not going to get tired of hearing our prayers. He loves us as his dear sons and daughters. Therefore, we should persevere in prayer for God to answer our requests!

2) <u>Pray with the right motives.</u>

> *When you ask, you do not receive, because you ask with the wrong motives, that you may spend what you get on your pleasures. (James 4:3)*

Sometimes we do indeed pray, but God seemingly does not answer. It could be that God "sees your motives." God does care about our motivations, and about why we ask him for something. We need to ask for a spouse for one reason only: to glorify God. We do not need to ask just for our selfish needs or emptiness. Brothers can adopt a very selfish attitude of wanting a wife to fulfill their sexual pleasures. God loves us too much to answer these kinds of impure prayers!

This is exactly what happened to Hannah in the Old Testament. She wanted a child badly, but God would not give her one, even though she prayed for many years. She was embittered towards God and towards life itself. Yet in the midst of her anguish, she offered God a special prayer. In the prayer she changed her motivations. Once she changed her motivations, God moved to grant her wishes because it was no longer for her but for God:

> *In her deep anguish Hannah prayed to the Lord, weeping bitterly. And she made a vow, saying "Lord Almighty, if you will only look on your servant's misery and remember me, and not forget your servant but give her a son, then I will give him to the Lord for all the days of his life, and no razor will ever be used on his head." (1 Samuel 1:10-11)*

After this prayer, God did something awesome! God gave her a child. And what a child! This was none other than the great prophet and last Judge of Israel, Samuel! God granted her prayer because the child was not for her anymore, but for God. She would have the child, and then she would give him away to be trained under Eli the priest, while the child was still very young. How hard this must have been for her! She gave up the child after he was weaned. But God was gracious to her and gave her five more children later. (1 Samuel 2:21) We can never out-give God, but he does want to see our motivations *". . . and disciplines us for our good, in order that we may share in his holiness."* *(Hebrews 12:10b)*

Why do we want to date and get married? Is it for us or is it for God? These are the questions we have to ask ourselves. When we make a decision to get married to glorify God, he will listen because he knows that we only want to glorify him.

   3) <u>Do not conform to the patterns of this world.</u>

> *Charm is deceptive, and beauty is fleeting;*
> *but a woman who fears the Lord is to be praised. (Proverbs 31:30)*

The Word of God explains to us what the most desirable trait in a woman should be. Amazingly, it is not looks but fear of the Lord! We are so enamored by looks in our society. In part, this is because physical beauty is what the world values. We are taught from a very young age to value it. We see it on television and in movies. Thanks be to God that this is not what God values. God values the heart, and especially the heart that fears the Lord. We try to be "spiritual" and say that this is not an important characteristic in choosing a husband and wife. Often times, we say the right thing with our words, but our actions betray us.

Physical beauty is so etched in our psyche as humans

that even the prophet Samuel fell for this when he was trying to anoint one of David's sons as the next King of Israel.

> *When they arrived, Samuel saw Eliab and thought, "Surely the Lord's anointed stands here before the Lord." But the Lord said to Samuel, "Do not consider his appearance or his height, for I have rejected him. The Lord does not look at the things people look at. People look at the outward appearance, but the Lord looks at the heart." (1 Samuel 16:6-7)*

This leads me to think about Jesus! We know that Jesus is God, but what were his physical characteristics? What did he look like? In the movies, we often see Jesus portrayed as blue-eyed and of light complexion with typical Hollywood looks. But was this so? The Bible says in Isaiah 52:2-3,

> *He had no beauty or majesty to attract us to him,*
> *nothing in his appearance that we should desire him.*
> *He was despised and rejected by mankind,*
> *a man of suffering, and familiar with pain.*
> *Like one from whom people hide their faces.*

Jesus was not physically attractive! There was no

beauty to attract us to him; nothing in his appearance made him desirable to people. Jesus could have chosen to come to this world in any physical form. Why choose an unattractive human form? After all, he was and is the King of Kings! What was God trying to teach us with this?

He was definitely trying to teach us what is really important, the spiritual qualities of a person as opposed to the physical ones. The physical qualities will go away in time anyway as we will all get old and lose our supposed "beauty." But our spiritual qualities are the ones that endure and by which we will be judged. These are the ones we should look for, in others and in ourselves.

In the area of looks, I think I have an advantage with my "lack of looks." As of this writing, I have been happily married for 17 years to my wife, Lynda. My wife certainly lives up to the Spanish meaning of her name "beautiful," as she is beautiful both inside and out! In my case, however, things are somewhat different from the external point of view.

Moreover, Lynda had never dated a Latin person before she became a Christian because she was not attracted to them or their culture. This alone shows that beauty and attraction are subjective to the individual. What one person finds attractive, others might not. I was not the typical person that Lynda would have been attracted to in the world. Yet as a Christian in the kingdom of God, she began to look for spiritual qualities instead of physical ones. This led her to want to date me, the first and only Latin person she dated and eventually married! I must say that I really appreciate the fact that she looked for spiritual qualities in a man as I am somewhat lacking in the physical ones that the world promotes so obsessively!

This is also one of the main reasons we sometimes do not date. We simply do not find people of the opposite sex according to our "standards." I have seen not a few brothers and sisters lose incredible opportunities in marrying a spiritual spouse who would ultimately take them to heaven because the person was not "their type." Many have lost the opportunity to be in the full-time ministry because of a wordly standard as well. I have also seen the opposite. I have seen brothers date and marry a sister because they were attracted to them, though the sister was spiritually weak at the time, only to find themselves in a living nightmare years later when the sister fell away from God, after they had kids to consider as well.

Also, if someone dates another person who is weak spiritually, but is very attracted to the person, the chances of being impure and immoral in those dating relationships are magnified because of their motivations. It is often the weak dating couples that tend to fall into sexual sin. The stronger the individuals are in the dating relationship, the higher the chance of staying pure because God is first and foremost in the relationship.

The problem is that we want everything to be perfect when it comes to the person we are going to date. We want the other person to be super-spiritual, super-attractive and with an incredible personality, and we decide to settle for nothing less. However, this thinking is not wise because we fail to consider one very important factor: We do not look at ourselves in the mirror! Are we super-spiritual, super-attractive and blessed with an incredible personality? Most likely we are not.

Let us have an accurate judgement of ourselves like it says in Romans 12:3,

> *For by the grace given me I say to every one of you: Do not think of yourself more highly than you ought, but rather think of yourself with sober judgement, in accordance with the faith God has distributed to each of you.*

If we are not "perfect," then let us not expect that from our future spouse! Do expect one thing and make no compromise in this area: The person you date and marry should love God with all their heart, mind, soul and strength!

I have heard it said many times, that choosing the person we marry is the second most important decision in our lives! This is absolutely true! Lately, though, I have heard a different saying, that choosing the person we marry is the most important decision we make in our lives as a disciple of Jesus! This is also true, as most of us make the decision to be a disciple before we get married. The person we date and marry will most likely be the one main determining factors of whether we will end up in heaven or hell.

We must be very prayerful and wise in whom we chose to date and get married!

4) <u>Seek advice.</u>

Interestingly, as Christians, we know the Scriptures that teach the importance of seeking advice. We can and we should seek advice in many areas of our Christian life, and that is very good. I have noticed that in the sentimental areas like dating and relationships, we tend to seek less advice because we tend to have more pride in these areas. Somehow, we think that we know what to do in this area. Yet, for a lot of us, it is precisely this area of our lives in which we have messed up the most. However, we can insist in thinking of having our own way in this area and not seeking any help. If we do so, we likely will get the same results we have received as a non-Christian. Someone once said that, "Insanity is doing the same things the same way and expecting different results." Let us not be insane but sane in our search for righteousness. I believe that we do not like advice in this area, because we know that we are going to hear something we do not like and that it will challenge our lives. Yet the Bible is true every time and does not change.

Though we have discussed this topic earlier, let us consider some more Scriptures about seeking advice:

> *Listen to advice and accept discipline, and at the end you will be counted among the wise. (Proverbs 19:20)*

The way of fools seems right to them, but the wise listen to advice. (Proverbs 12:15)

For lack of guidance a nation falls, but victory is won through many advisers. (Proverbs 11:14)

Where there is strife, there is pride, but wisdom is found in those who take advice. (Proverbs 13:10)

Listen to advice and accept discipline, and at the end you will be counted among the wise. (Proverbs 19:20)

I thank God that in my Christian life, I have had many godly men and women who have advised me in this important area. I have had mentors (disciplers) who have helped mold my thinking in this area. These were married men in the church who had great marriages and a great walk with God. These were men whose godly characteristics I wanted to imitate.

The next step is how to keep the dating relationship pure while we are in it. We need to accept discipline in this area. We need to impose on ourselves parameters in order to stay pure. We should discuss these parameters with other disciples to keep us accountable. What are parameters? They are self-imposed rules that we abide by in order to protect us and others from falling into sexual sin.

Here are some examples:

1) <u>Never be alone together:</u> If we are dating in the kingdom, we should try to never be alone with our girlfriend in an apartment or a house. It is not that something sexual is necessarily going to happen, it is just a precautionary mechanism so that nothing does indeed happen.

2) <u>Have a phone curfew:</u> Another wise parameter is not to talk late at night with our girlfriend or boyfriend as our guard tends to be down at this time because we are tired. Of course there are exceptions to this. Yet generally speaking, when it is late at night we are more tempted to say improper, sensual or sexual things.

3) <u>Say quick goodbyes:</u> The time when we are saying goodbye to our girlfriend or boyfriend and leaving him or her at the house is also a time of temptation. I recommend saying goodbye quickly because emotions can get us at this point and we can hug or kiss inappropriately because of the sheer emotion of leaving someone we like so much.

4) <u>Go on double dates:</u> We also always need to go on double dates when we go out because of the potential impurity that there is when we are alone. It is not, as said *before, that something impure will happen but* simply to guard against the potential for something impure happening. It is not sin to go on a date by ourselves. It is an issue of spiritual protection because we are both attracted to each other.

All of these parameters can be summed up in one Scripture:

> *I have the right to do anything, you say – but not everything is beneficial. "I have the right to do anything" – but not everything is constructive. No one should seek their own good, but the good of others. (1 Corinthians 10:23-24)*

Here are some other dating parameters:

- <u>Not kissing on the lips:</u> About kissing, I recommend that dating couples do not kiss each other on the lips as that can lead to other things like kissing sensually and/or touching inappropriately. Best not to kiss at all, and the first kiss be at the altar!

- <u>Side hugs are best:</u> About hugging, I recommend as a parameter to stay away from full frontal hugs as we can feel each other's private parts, inadvertently, when we do this.

These and others are among some of the parameters Lynda and I had when we were dating, and they were definitely key in us having the pure dating relationship we were blessed to have.

We might say that these parameters are somewhat extreme and that we do not need them, and that we can perfectly control ourselves. We may have the strength to control ourselves sensually and sexually, but we forget one thing: How about our brothers and sisters? Maybe they do not have the self-control that we have. It is selfish to think just in terms of what benefits only ourselves and not to think about others and their weaknesses. Besides, no one is strong according to the Word of God. We may have success in our purity ten times in a row doing something unwise just to fall the eleventh time, because we decided to trust in ourselves.

In conclusion, starting an awesome dating relationship with someone we wind up marrying and having an awesome marriage is an issue of faith. That is totally up to us. In this chapter, we have seen some spiritual principles of how God can accomplish this very important thing in our lives. Please take the challenge to apply these principles, and watch God work.

Chapter 24
The Battle Won With The Power Of The Holy Spirit

In this final chapter, we will look at how the power of the Holy Spirit of God can help us overcome sexual sin. Let us consider this Scripture:

> *The mind governed by the flesh is hostile to God; it does not submit to God's law, nor can it do so. You, however, are not in the realm of the flesh but are in the realm of the Spirit of Christ, they do not belong to Christ.*
>
> *The mind governed by the flesh is hostile to God; it does not submit to God's law, nor can it do so. Those who are in the realm of the flesh cannot please God.*
>
> *You, however, are not in the realm of the flesh but are in the realm of the Spirit, if indeed the Spirit of God lives in you. And if anyone does not have the Spirit of Christ, they do not belong to Christ. (Romans 8:7-9)*

To belong to Christ, we need to have the Spirit of God living in us. If we do not have the Holy Spirit, we cannot submit to God's law. That means that if we do not have the Spirit of God, we cannot obey God even if we try to. Paul, inspired by the Holy Spirit, writes to the Romans that our mind is governed by the flesh.

It is the Holy Spirit of God that gives us the power to overcome sin, and in the case of the focus of this book, sexual sin. I think about myself as an example. Before I was converted at the age of 22, I was enslaved to masturbation. I could not change. I could not stop doing it. I tried stopping, and the most that I was able to go without it was about one week. After I was converted to Christ and received the Holy Spirit, I never masturbated again and was happily married to the love of my life, Lynda, at the age of 27. That means that for five years, I did not masturbate. Now that is a miracle! I went from not being able to stop doing it for five days to going without any sexual activity for five years. Without a doubt, it was the power of the Holy Spirit that gave me this great victory. I knew, without a doubt, that I had the Holy Spirit because it was impossible for me to change on my own power. We can only change through the power of the Holy Spirit.

That means that if we are not true Christians, we cannot change. If you are reading this book and not a true converted disciple of Jesus, all the practicals in this book will be of little avail to us. The way for us to overcome sexual sin is first to be converted Biblically to Jesus. Then, and only then, can we embark on the challenge of changing and overcoming sexual sin.

Many reading this book are true disciples of Christ but have not seen the victories in our purity that we and God would like to see. Why does this happen? How can a truly converted disciple of Jesus live a life of impurity and sexual sin? Unfortunately, it is possible.

Let us consider the following passage of Scripture:

> ***Therefore, brothers and sisters, we have an obligation – but it is not to the flesh, to live according to it. For if you live according to the flesh, you will die; but if by the Spirit you put to death the misdeeds of the body, you will live. (Romans 8:12-13)***

This is a very interesting Scripture. It states that with the Spirit we can put to death the misdeeds of the body. Here lies a spiritual principle: The Spirit does not make us spiritual but gives us the potential to be spiritual. We can have the Spirit and not be spiritual and live in sin. This is why many Christians live in sexual sin and cannot seem to change. We have the Spirit of Christ living in us, but we are not utilizing it to change and overcome our sin.

We know that the non-Christian who does not have the Spirit cannot be spiritual and obey God. However, the true Christian can. That does not mean that he or she will. How can we utilize the power of the Spirit to overcome sexual sin? The answer lies in being full of the Holy Spirit. When we are full of the Holy Spirit, we do not have room to sin.

Here we see another important spiritual principle: Christians have the Holy Spirit living in them, but they are not necessarily full of the Spirit! To be full of the Spirit requires us to make a decision to be full of the Holy Spirit. It is a spiritual discipline that we need to develop, and it does not come naturally. Only through spiritual discipline can we overcome sexual sin because our power over sin is not enough. We need God's power.

These are four practical decisions we can make daily to be full of the Holy Spirit:

1) Pray radically.

> *Now, lord, consider their threats and enable your servants to speak your word with great boldness. Stretch out your hand to heal and perform signs and wonders through the name of your holy servant, Jesus.*
>
> *After they prayed, the place where they were meeting was shaken. And they were all filled with the Holy Spirit and spoke the word of God boldly. (Acts 4:29-31)*

The first spiritual principle is: When we pray radically, we become full of the Holy Spirit! This is awesome, and herein lies our problem. We pray, but we often do not pray radically and are thus not full of the Holy Spirit. Being full of the Holy Spirit is a special power and enthusiasm that comes from God when we pray radically. If we do not pray radically, we will not be full of the Holy Spirit, and then we will be left wondering why we are not happy or fired up to face the challenges of our day and be pure for

God. Jesus prayed radically even though he was God in the flesh!

During the days of Jesus's life on earth, he offered up prayers and petitions with fervent cries and tears to the one who could save him from death, and he was heard because of his reverent submission. (Hebrews 5:7)

If Jesus prayed with loud cries and tears, how much more should we? But we do not, and that is why we fail in the area of purity. We are not full of the Holy Spirit and thus fall to temptation. If we are not overcoming sexual sin, it is because our prayers are weak and not consistent. We need to get on our knees and lock ourselves in a room. Then we need to pray with all our heart. We need to get loud and intense when we pray as we approach God. We need sometimes to sweat. It is an exercise to pray radically. Only then will we be temporarily full of the Holy Spirit and thus have the power to overcome sexual sin. Then, the next day, we need to do the same thing.

An obvious challenge is finding a place to pray with loud cries and tears. I believe God makes this hard on purpose because he wants to see to what lengths we will go to pray to him radically. Jesus had to climb mountains and go to solitary places. What lengths will we go to pray radically to God so we can be filled with the Holy Spirit?

It is not easy for me as I live in an apartment building, and I have kids and live in the huge metropolitan city of Sao Paulo. There are people everywhere. Yet I try with all my heart to make it happen, because I need to be filled with the Holy Spirit.

Something to note is the issue of prayer walks. Even though I am not against prayer walks, but at least for me it is very hard to pray with loud cries and tears on a prayer walk unless I am in a remote area. One is going to look crazy to bystanders if one is praying loud as one walks and there are people nearby.

The challenge is clear: Pray radically, and we will be filled with the Holy Spirit.

2) <u>Sing to God radically.</u>

Do not get drunk on wine, which leads to debauchery. Instead, be filled with the Spirit, speaking to one another with psalms, hymns, and songs from the Spirit. Sing and make music from your heart to the Lord. (Ephesians 5:18-19)

I love this Scripture! Singing radically to the Lord fills us with the Holy Spirit, not just singing but singing radically. I believe music was created to worship God! Music moves the soul. It is a spiritual phenomenon. I believe the birds sing to God. In the city of Sao Paulo, we use the subway as a mode of transportation because it is so busy. Amazingly, yet not surprisingly, most travelers in the subway are listening to music on their phones. Why? Music moves the soul whether we are Christian or not. Satan knows this, and he takes advantage of this, giving us music that damages the soul.

Notwithstanding, making *"music from our hearts to the Lord"* radically fills us up with the Holy Spirit. Just singing in a lukewarm way will not fill us up with the Holy Spirit. We have to sing with all our heart and soul. There is no excuse not to sing to the person we love most: That is God! Some just listen to the songs at church. That will not fill us up with the Spirit. Some say that they do not know the lyrics. That is why we have song books. Others say that they do not have a good voice. It does not matter. God does not care. That is why the Scripture says:

Make a joyful noise unto the Lord, all ye lands. (Psalm 100:1 KJV)

Sing with joy to the Lord with all our hearts and do not worry about the quality of our voice. Worry about the quality of our hearts. Then, we will be full of the Holy Spirit, albeit temporarily, and we will definitely be more prepared to tackle any temptation in the sexual area!

3) Love the Word of God radically.

"When he was at the table with them, he took bread, gave thanks, broke it and began to give it to them. Then their eyes were opened and they recognized him, and he disappeared from their sight. They asked each other, Were not our hearts burning within us while he talked with us on the road and opened the Scriptures to us?" *(Luke 24:30-32)*

After Jesus left the two disciples that he met on the road to Emmaus, the disciples' hearts were *"burning"* as Jesus explained to them the prophetic Messianic Scriptures. The *"burning"* is not physical but spiritual. Their hearts were full of the Spirit because they were full of the Word of God.

Another way to get full of the Holy Spirit is to love the Word of God radically. When we are full of the Word of God, we are full of the Spirit of God and thus we can overcome sexual sins and any other sins.

Blessed is the one who does not walk in step with the wicked
Or stand in the way that sinners take
or sit in the company of mockers, but
whose delight is in the law of the Lord,
and who meditates on his law day and night. (Psalm 1:1-2)

235

When we delight in the law of the Lord both day and night, we will not be in the company of sinners nor will we have the time for it. This is an incredible privilege that we have as disciples, to know and to love God's Word, to meditate on it, and to think deeply about it. The Word of God will change us, if we love it radically and treasure it in our hearts.

The great majority of disciples who struggle with sexual sins do not love the Word of God radically or even talk about it. This is precisely why they struggle. They are not full of the Holy Spirit. They are full of themselves.

I recommend memorizing Scriptures and reading the whole Bible once a year. I also recommend studying the Bible with a journal in hand. With that, we can write the insights that God has taught us that day. Then, we can reference back to them in the future both to help ourselves and other disciples. This has been my practice for 20 years, and it has saved my spiritual life and my purity.

The Bible never ceases to be amazing. Let us meditate on some passages about the Word of God in Psalm 119,

How can a young person stay on the path of purity? By living according to your word. (v. 10)

I have hidden your Word in my heart that I might not sin against you. (v. 11)

I rejoice in following your statutes as one rejoices in great riches. (v. 14)

Open my eyes that I may see wonderful things in your law. (v. 18)

For I delight in your commands because I love them. (v. 47)

My comfort in my suffering is this: Your promise preserves my life. (v. 50)

Your Word, Lord, is eternal; it stands firm in the heavens. (v. 89)

To all perfection I see a limit, but your commands are boundless. (v. 96)

Oh, how I love your law! I meditate on it all day long. (v. 97)

I have more insight than all my teachers, for I meditate on your statutes. (v. 99)

Great peace have those who love your law, and nothing can make them stumble. (v. 165)

As Christians, we need to cultivate a genuine amazement towards God's Words. We need to be in awe of how amazing God's Word really is. This is the key! We can be fired up about a sporting event or about a musical band that we like. Yet where is the man that is fired up about God's eternal Word? That man, and that man only, will be able to stay sexually pure in this godless and defiled world!

4) Love the mission radically.

The mission that God has given us is a great one. We are to evangelize the world in our generation just like the disciples did in their generation. (Matthew 28:18-20)

Let us look at the following Scripture:

The Word of the Lord spread through the whole region. But the Jewish leaders incited the God-fearing women of high standing and the leading men of the city. They stirred up persecution against Paul and Barnabas, and expelled them from their region. So they shook the dust off their feet as a warning to them and went to Iconium. And the disciples were filled with joy and with the Holy Spirit. (Acts 13:49-52)

The disciples effectively evangelized the whole region of Pisidian Antioch. This evangelistic success came because they received persecution as any disciple who preaches the Word of God. Everyone heard of Jesus not because Christians shared with them, but because they heard persecuation. Nonetheless, the passage says that the Christians were full of joy and of the Holy Spirit. Why were they full of joy and of the Holy Spirit? They were carrying out the mission to seek and save the lost.

When we love the mission radically, we are full of the Holy Spirit and thus are full of joy. This joy comes from seeing how God changes people through his gospel. We see people repent from all their sins including sexual sins. This, in fact, gives us even more conviction to stay pure. We do not have time, and neither do we want to mess with any sexual sin or any kind of impurity, because we are busy with the Lord's work. This will happen, because we are full of the Spirit.

Brothers and sisters that are idle in the mission tend to be impure because they are selfish. When we are sacrificing our time, money and energy to save the lost, we will be full of joy and of the Holy Spirit and we will be pure.

I recommend sharing our faith every day with non-Christians, not just one person per day. From time to time setting a goal that pushes our faith and our comfort zone so that others can be saved is recommended as well, not only sharing our faith daily but getting into Bible studies with non-Christians weekly. This is indeed one of the great purposes that God has given us to do in this dark and corrupt world, to change this world for Jesus Christ. If we do this, we will be filled with joy and the Holy Spirit!

We can overcome any and all sexual sin when we are full of the Holy Spirit. By ourselves we cannot do it, but with God we gain the victory in this sad world where sexual sin and promiscuity are rapidly increasing. The answer to impurity is God. It has always been God. It will always be God. Our relationship with Him is what helps us to change in this area. Winning the battle of sexual purity is possible with God, and there are many examples of Christians who have overcome their sexual sins through the power of the Holy Spirit.

Looking back at David, Solomon and Samson, we see three leaders that were not able, at first, to overcome their sexual temptations. It was, indeed, a battle that even kings lost! What is ironic is that they were "men of God." They are heroes in the Bible! When we think about David, we see, "a man after God's heart," who happened to sin greatly! The greatest thing, however, is that he repented. This is what makes him a man after God's heart. Righteousness is not being perfect. Rather, righteousness is defined by how we respond when we sin and fall short. (Proverbs 24:16) As we saw in Chapter 15, David changed and was never adulterous again. He restored his relationship with God and with his wife, Bathsheba. The same thing can be said about Bathsheba. As bad as their sin was, they repented and God forgave them. This is part of what makes the Bible awesome. We get an up-close look at Bible heroes who sinned and then repented. They were not perfect. In fact, they were just like us. Since they were just like us, we can muster faith and courage from their example to do the same. If David changed, we too can change! If David repented, we too can repent!

When we look at King Solomon, we also see repentance. After all his sin, when he was old, he wrote the book of Ecclesiastes. As an old man, he finishes this delightful book of wisdom with these words:

> *Of making many books there is no end, and much study wearies the body. Now all has been heard; here is the conclusion of the matter: Fear God and keep his commandments, for this is the duty of all mankind. For God will bring every deed into judgment, including every hidden thing, whether it is good or evil. (Ecclesiastes 12:12-14)*

Solomon understood what was important in life. It took him almost an entire lifetime, but in the end he got it! Some of us can relate to him. From these verses we can see that Solomon finally had a deep fear of God, understood obedience and judgement, as well as the vanity in trying to conceal sin. We can confidently say that he repented, which is remarkable when you consider that he probably was the person who sinned the most, sexually, in all the Bible! If he was able to change, we can change. And like the saying goes, "It is better late than never."

Praise God that we know that Samson made it to heaven! His hair grew back, his super-natural strength returned, and he sacrificed himself to kill 3,000 of God's enemies!

Regardless of the lives of these men, we now need to ask ourselves a very serious question: How is your purity? Will it remain inconclusive? I hope not! You have the ability to change, to repent, to forgive and to be an amazing man or woman of God! Will there be a lack openness on your part to deal with it? Will there be a lack of information? I really hope not. I hope and pray that this book has been beneficial as we studied many of the Scriptures in the Bible that have to do with sexual purity. Let us learn from the lives of these powerful men. Do not let their examples be in vain, but make a decision to learn from their mistakes and imitate their righteousness. This is no longer a battle to be lost. It is a battle to be won! I really hope and pray that you make a decision to be pure today and for the rest of your life! Then and only then, we will win the battle of sexual purity, and to God be the glory!

Bibliography

Chapter One
Stanton, Glenn. What is the actual US divorce rate and risk? Lifesitenews.com. Family, Marriage, Wed Dec 23, 2015.

Chapter 10
Merriam-Webster. Merriam-Webster.com/dictionary/metanoia. 2017 Merriam-Webster, Incorporated.

Chapter 13
Merriam-Webster. Merriam-Webster.com/dictionary/psalm. 2017 Merriam-Webster, Incorporated.

Chapter 16
The Huffington Post. *Porn Sites Get More Visitors Each Month Than Netflix, Amazon And Twitter Combined.* huffpostbrasil.com/entry/internet-porn-stats_n_3187682. 04/05/2013.

Chapter 18
Hammond, Guy. *Caring Beyond the Margins (What Every Christian Needs to Know About Homosexuality).* Illumination Publishers, 2012.

Made in the USA
Middletown, DE
20 August 2018